Proactive Deaf Education:

Cognitive Socialization

John Muma and Henry Teller, Editors

Butte Publications, Inc.
Hillsboro, Oregon, U.S.A.

Proactive Deaf Education: Cognitive Socialization

John Muma and Henry Teller, Editors

Design and Layout: Anita Jones

Butte Publications, Inc.
P. O. Box 1328
Hillsboro, OR 97123-1328
U.S.A.

ISBN 1-884362-64-8

To my daughter, Taylor Muma.

J.R.M.

To my parents, Henry and Jeane Teller;
my wife, Carol; my children, Henry III and Sarah;
and my stepfather, Alvin Aydell.

H.E.T.

Contents

About the Authors

Sharon Baker is an associate professor of deaf education at the University of Tulsa. She received her doctorate in curriculum and instruction from Oklahoma State University. She is the co-author of *Language Learning in Children Who Are Deaf and Hard of Hearing: Multiple Pathways*. Dr. Baker has years of experience teaching deaf children at both the elementary and secondary levels. In 1992 she received the Lee Katz Memorial Award from the American Society for Deaf Children.

Steven J. Cloud is an assistant professor at the University of Southern Mississippi. He received his undergraduate degree in communication disorders from Western Carolina University and his master's degree from the University of South Carolina. He graduated from the University of Tennessee–Knoxville with a Ph.D. in 1997. Dr. Cloud's primary interest is in multicultural language issues, but he also teaches courses in adult neurogenics, dysphagia, stuttering, and anatomy and physiology of the speech mechanism.

Susan R. Easterbrooks is a professor in the department of educational psychology and special education at Georgia State University. Educated at University of Connecticut, Emory University, and the University of Georgia, she has served in the field for almost three decades as a teacher, psychometrist, administrator, lecturer, author, and researcher. Dr. Easterbrooks has been active on many national committees, including the National Board for Professional Standards' Exceptional Needs Committee and CEC's Division for Communicative Disabilities and Deafness. She co-authored *Language Learning in Children Who Are Deaf and Hard of Hearing: Multiple Pathways*.

Fran Hagstrom is an assistant professor in the department of rehabilitation, human resource, and communication disorders at the University of Arkansas–Fayetteville. She received her doctorate in developmental psychology from Clark University. Dr. Hagstrom's sociocultural approach to cognitive communication research focuses on contextualized problem solving, attending, and remembering.

John Muma is a professor of speech and hearing sciences at the University of Southern Mississippi. He has made over 200 presentations, including 40 featured-speaker presentations to state speech and hearing conventions. He has over 70 publications, including five books. Dr. Muma is an ASHA fellow and received the ASHA President's Council Award of Excellence for his work in developing the Cognitive Socialization clinical model.

Henry Teller is an associate professor and director of the Education of the Deaf program in the department of speech and hearing sciences at the University of Southern Mississippi. He completed graduate studies in deaf education and special education at the University of Alabama and the University of Southern California. Dr. Teller has worked in the area of deaf education as a teacher and teacher educator for over 30 years. He has published numerous articles and book chapters and given many presentations, most focused on the development of English literacy with students who are deaf or hard of hearing.

Alfred H. White, Jr., received his B.S. and M.S. from the University of Utah and his Ph.D. from Michigan State University. He has served as a classroom teacher, a parent-infant advisor, and as the assistant principal and director of curriculum and research at the Maryland School for the Deaf. He has written language curriculum for the state of Texas and currently is a professor and chair of the department of communication sciences and disorders at Texas Woman's University.

Preface

Deaf education has made numerous claims for being proactive. Given the developments in cognitive socialization over the past decade and their forthcoming impacts on special education possibly in accordance with the **National Agenda**, it behooves deaf education to turn to this literature toward becoming proactive. There are two motivations for doing so:

> *Developments in cognitive socialization*

(a) the third-generation advancements in the cognition and language acquisition literatures with the substantive issues attendant to this generation; and (b) the potential changes in special education attendant to the **National Agenda**.

There are three discernible generations in the cognitive and language acquisition literatures. They are described as follows:

- **Traditional Generation:** authoritarianism, traditional grammar (parts of speech, sentence types), expressive and receptive modalities and cuing, associationism, habit strength, reinforcement,

  > *Three generations*

  frequency counts, percentages, age and grade levels, checklists, phonology (initial, medial, and final consonants and omissions, substitutions, and distortions)
- **Psycholinguistic Generation:** generative grammar, learnability; cognitive precursors; acquisition sequences; explicit content, implicit content; form-content-use, pregrammatical and grammatical children
- **Cognitive Socialization Generation:** centrality of intent, social commerce, government and binding grammar, possible worlds, situated minds, mimesis, repertoire, contextual evidence, active loci, socialization, parallel talk, socialization and peer modeling, and communicative payoff

Roger Brown (1956) was right! Language acquisition is "a process of cognitive socialization" (p. 247). The cognitive socialization literature, especially over the previous decade, has yielded many (about forty) major substantive changes in understanding both cognitive

> *Recent developments in cognitive socialization*

and language acquisition (Cloud & Muma, 1999). Accordingly, special educators in general, and deaf educators in particular, may want to alter some of their views and practices to become aligned with the cognitive socialization literature.

The **National Agenda** is a proactive effort to upgrade the educational services for the deaf and hard of hearing. The central issue for the **National Agenda** is communication. The extent to which the **National Agenda** becomes linked with the substantive

National Agenda

issues in the cognitive socialization literature is the extent to which this agenda has a chance of making major contributions toward appropriate educational services for individuals who are deaf or hard of hearing.

Consistent with the ASHA Training Standards (Rees & Snope, 1983), the cognitive socialization literature is based on the philosophical views of constructionism (Searle, 1992), functionalism (Bates & MacWhinney, 1979), relevance theory (Sperber & Wilson, 1986), bootstrapping theory (Gleitman, 1994; Pinker, 1987), and learnability theory (Pinker, 1988). Brief summaries of these views and perspectives are provided in Appendix A. These views and perspectives provide disciplined understandings derived from the attendant scholarly literatures toward establishing appropriate rationales for services in deaf education.

Philosophical views and theoretical perspectives

Such understandings go a long way toward overcoming arbitrary, capricious, authoritarian, and dogmatic positions that characterize the traditional generation and remain evidenced to some extent today. Thus, proactive deaf education should strive to become aligned with the cognitive socialization generation.

This generation provides about forty major new developments in the literature. Appendix B lists the forty major developments. Accordingly, it behooves the fields of special education in general, and deaf education, speech-language pathology, and learning disabilities in particular, to incorporate these issues in their views and activities. This, of course, means that these professional fields need to learn about the substantive

Forty major new developments

issues and how to implement them into appropriate teaching strategies and services. The purpose of this book is to present basic substantive issues emanating from the cognitive socialization literature so that the field of deaf education can take a proactive position in rendering more appropriate services to individuals who are deaf and hard of hearing.

Perhaps we should recognize the recent major **Catalyst Grant** that was provided to the field of deaf education for advancing the field via technology. Word processing and Internet searches of various kinds were instrumental, opening new substantive vistas in the cognitive socialization literature. Thus, this grant has played a significant role

Catalyst Grant: Opening new substantive vistas

in helping educators appreciate new developments in the cognitive socialization literature.

This book begins with a general position statement derived from constructionism because this philosophical view was deemed more coherent than several other views (Searle, 1992). The book also focuses on relevance theory and bootstrapping theory because these perspectives were identified by the editor of the *Journal of Child Language* (Perera, 1994) as two of the most influential perspectives over the previous twenty-five years. It then addresses major substantive issues, several of which are predicated on the centrality of intent (Bruner, 1986; Searle, 1983).

Constructionism to relevance and bootstrapping theories

Various chapters address these and other substantive issues with their attendant applications for deaf education. This book is intended as a vehicle to launch the field of deaf education into the substantive base of cognitive socialization toward providing more effective teaching for individuals who are deaf and hard of hearing. Thus, it is intended to usher deaf education into the cognitive socialization perspective.

As deaf education strives to be a scholarly profession, it is necessary to become oriented on the relevant philosophical views and theoretical perspectives in the scholarly literature. Toward this end, deaf education should become familiar with the philosophical view of constructionism and the speech act, relevance, and bootstrapping theoretical perspectives. These views and perspectives are summarized in Appendix A.

With these views and perspectives, it becomes necessary to question several popular views and practices, notably the modality view (expressive/receptive modalities), reinforcement theory, frequency measurements, reliance on structure rather than function, and psychometric normative tests. Furthermore, it is necessary to address the heterogeneous nature of the deaf and hard of hearing populations. Technology may play an increasingly important role in providing appropriate educational services to the deaf and hard of hearing populations.

⌐ Chapter 1 ¬
Proactive Deaf Education: Cognitive Socialization

John Muma, Ph.D., and Henry Teller, Ed.D.
University of Southern Mississippi

The title of this book is rather bold. It is bold because it presumes the existence of a substantive scholarly base for becoming proactive. And it is bold because numerous individuals in higher education have expressed a desire for deaf education to become proactive as evidenced by the **National Agenda.**

Becoming proactive

Proactive ventures are earned. Such ventures are not invested in individuals but in disciplines that have earned such privileges by virtue of a solid scholarly base. Thus, the desire to become proactive hinges on the extent to which a given field evidences a solid scholarly base.

Scholarly base

This means that a field needs to become introspective concerning its various substantive issues to ascertain the degree to which it is driven by scholarship or politics. Such introspection goes directly to the philosophical views and theoretical perspectives that underwrite a field. Several views and perspectives are summarized in Appendix A. The penetrating question becomes: Which scholarly views and perspectives underwrite deaf education?

Introspection

Inasmuch as the field of deaf education is an applied field, the subsequent question becomes: What are the conceptual and operational implications of these views and perspectives for individuals who are deaf or hard of hearing?

Deaf education: Views and perspectives

Two somewhat unrelated issues that may be driving forces in the consideration of philosophical views and theoretical views are: (a) the heterogeneous

Heterogeneity and technology

nature of special education populations, and (b) the role of advancing technology in the present era.

Views and Perspectives

Before addressing these issues, it is necessary to consider the purpose of philosophical views and theoretical perspectives. By understanding these purposes, it becomes apparent that bona fide professional organizations strive to establish their views and perspectives aligned with the available scholarly literature. By doing so, a profession not only becomes elevated to a contemporary stance but also dethrones authoritarianism, capriciousness, dogma, hype, impressionism, and misused eclecticism.

Understanding the purposes or functions of philosophical views and theoretical perspectives provides justifications for orienting a field or profession in particular ways. Special education in general, and deaf education in particular, are in need of bona fide philosophical views simply because these fields are currently operating essentially without such views. Indeed, many professionals in special education have taken the view that they do not want to be bothered by philosophical views and theoretical perspectives.

The purpose of **philosophical views** is to provide coherent points of view or frameworks. Because of coherence, such views provide a rationale for holding particular views and rendering particular practices. The key, then, is coherence toward establishing justifiable rationales for rendering appropriate services. This is crucial for special education because the central issue in the federal legislation is that each child is entitled to the most appropriate education and services.

> *Philosophical views: Provide coherent points of view*

Searle (1992), the foremost scholar in the philosophy of cognition and language, critiqued the degree of coherence for the following philosophical views: behaviorism, monism, dualism, materialism, reductionism, functionalism, and constructionism. He showed that the latter two views were the most coherent.

Constructionism is more strongly evident in the scholarly cognition and language acquisition literatures than any of the other views. Constructionism holds that an individual is an active processor of information and that an

> *Constructionism: Active processing*

individual's capacities are governed to a large extent by his or her available repertoire, progress in acquisition sequences, strategies of learning, and active loci of learning. The implication is that teachers of the deaf should ascertain these domains to facilitate active learning (Muma, 1978, 1986, 1998).

Functionalism is also prominent in the scholarly language acquisition literature. Functionalism holds that the structures of language serve its functions. Language has both cognitive and communicative functions. The main **cognitive functions** are repre-

> *Functionalism: Cognitive and communicative functions*

sentation (Mandler, 1983) and mediation (Nelson, 1996). The act of verbalizing provides a means of representing experience that in turn establishes an individual's possible worlds (Bruner, 1986) or situated minds (Nelson, 1996). Furthermore, such verbalizations may mediate or induce new insights or perspectives toward problem solving (Karmiloff-Smith, 1992; Nelson, 1996) and categorization (Mandler, 1983).

There are two main **communicative functions**: intent and content. Intent is the purpose of communication. Messages are constructed so that intent becomes recognizable (Grice, 1975; Sperber & Wilson, 1986). There are two kinds of content: explicit and implicit. Explicit content is the basic ideas entailed in messages. For example, the

> *Messages make intent recognizable.*

sentence "She wants a soft drink" contains these basic ideas: Someone wants something. Furthermore, messages may be verbal and/or nonverbal. Implicit content refers to an individual's knowledge of the world that enables him or her to deal with explicit content. For example, the following message does not make sense unless the reader has implicit knowledge of the field of antique fishing tackle: "I would like a Heddon crackleback 300." The implication is that it is necessary to establish a rich and varied experiential, social, and emotional base to enable an individual with appropriate implicit content so that explicit content works as intended to recognize intent. The implications for deaf education is that it is necessary to continually vary and expand an individual's experiential, social, and emotional worlds and that intent should comprise the bases of language acquisition. These issues constitute a major shift in the

> *Implicit content: possible worlds; explicit content: basic ideas entailed in messages*

education of deaf and hard of hearing individuals toward more accomplished communication and literacy.

There are three purposes for **theoretical perspectives:** understanding, explanation, and prediction (Kaplan, 1964). And there are three respective levels of evaluating the adequacies of theories: descriptive adequacy, explanatory adequacy, and empirical adequacy (Bohannon & Bonvillian, 2001; Chomsky, 1957). Theories obtain **descriptive adequacy** toward explaining a particular domain when they meet the following criteria (Tunkis, 1963): simple, complete, formal, and noncontradictory. In regard to language, a theoretical model must be simple by virtue of eliminating excess complexity. It must be complete by not leaving out crucial aspects. It must be formal by accounting for abstraction, representation, and the organization underlying language. It must be noncontradictory because it cannot have one aspect contradict another aspect.

> *Theories provide explanations, understandings, and predictions.*

> *Descriptive adequacy: simple, complete, formal, and noncontradictory evidence*

Explanatory adequacy for language can be achieved in one or both of the following ways: mental accounts or developmental accounts. The extent to which a theory of grammar accounts for the ways in which an individual functions mentally or cognitively is the extent to which a theory achieves explanatory adequacy. The four levels of the cognitive social bases of language are (Muma, 1986, 1998):

> *Explanatory adequacy: mental processing or acquisition sequences*

a. cognitive base (possible worlds, situated mind)
b. substantive issues specific to language (intent, explicit and implicit content)
c. mental processing that is not modality-specific (Clark & Clark, 1977; Karmiloff-Smith, 1992; Tallal, 1990)
d. metalinguistic awareness

> *Cognitive social bases of language*

Developmental accounts pertain to progress in acquisition sequences, strategies of learning, and active loci of learning. The extent to which a theory is compatible with these issues is the extent to which it achieves some measure of explanatory adequacy.

Empirical adequacy is the act of obtaining data that support or refute a particular theory. Data that are not theory-driven are nothing more than brute empiricism. Such atheoretical data are a threat to scholarship simply because they could be interpreted capriciously. Capricious stances such as misused eclecticism undermine scholarship.

> *Empirical adequacy: data that support or refute theories*

Baggage: Legacies

With these considerations and the need for a profession to maintain a scholarly stance, it becomes necessary to identify old policies, issues, and practices that are no longer supported by the scholarly literature. Toward that end, approximately forty traditional notions, views, and practices in special education in general and speech-language pathology, deaf education, and learning disabilities have been identified that lack support in the contemporary scholarly literature (Cloud & Muma, 1999; Muma, 1998). High on the list of issues that lack support are the following:

> *The need to question forty major issues*

a. modality view of language (expressive/receptive; auditory/visual)
b. reinforcement theory (behaviorism)
c. structure independent of function
d. language tests that lack construct validity from a theoretical perspective

Muma (1986) showed that none of the major language scholars such as Bloom, Brown, Bruner, Cazden, Chomsky, Grice, Nelson, Pinker, Snow, Sperber, and Wilson have held a modality view of language. Accordingly, one would be hard-pressed to find many modality-oriented articles in the *Journal of Child Language* over the past four decades. It is instructive to note that these scholars have held the core CCCE (cognition, codification, communication, expression; Muma, 1978, 1986, 1998) view. Thus, the extent to which a profession continues to hold the modality view is the extent to which it may be disconnected from the contemporary scholarly literature.

> *The modality view misses the core CCCE issues.*

The modality view was proposed by Osgood (1957) and applied in the *Illinois Test of Psycholinguistic Abilities* (Kirk, McCarthy, & Kirk, 1968). Special education, speech-language pathology, and deaf education adopted these perspectives. Unfortunately, the modality view had a short life span in the scholarly literature. The emergence of speech acts theory (Grice, 1975; Searle, 1969) and subsequently relevance theory (Sperber & Wilson, 1986), plus the comprehensive review of the literature (Clark & Clark, 1977) attendant to language production (planning and execution) and comprehension (construction and utilization) made it abundantly clear that modality information is "purged" early in information processing, with the bulk of mental activities in language operating on the prepositional nature of an intended message. Accordingly, the major language acquisition scholars have long since dropped the modality view and turn to the language CCCE core (Muma, 1986, 1998).

> *Modality aspects are purged in information processing.*

It should be abundantly clear that reinforcement theory was not one of the five most influential theories of language acquisition over the past three decades or so that were identified by Perera (1994). Reinforcement has not held up to the criteria of descriptive adequacy, explanatory adequacy, or empirical adequacy. Kohn (1993) and Searle (1992) have provided the most thorough accounts of the failings of reinforcement theory. And reinforcement theory has been silent about the centrality of intent, progress in acquisition sequences, strategies of learning, and active loci of learning. Perhaps two quotes from major language scholars will suffice: "Models of language acquisition built explicitly on assumptions of positive and negative reinforcement are no longer acceptable" (Nelson, 1985, p. 33), and "The absurdity of behaviorism lies in the fact that it denies the existence of any mental states" (Searle, 1992, p. 35).

> *Reinforcement does not provide a viable account of learning.*

Unfortunately, the most that can be said for reinforcement theory as an agent of language acquisition is that it makes teachers and clinicians operational. It gives them something to do under the guise of language acquisition. In this arena, such practices fall embarrassingly short of scholarly accounts of language acquisition. Kohn (1993) and Searle (1992)

> *Reinforcement makes teachers operational.*

have provided the most comprehensive accounts of the limitations of behaviorism and reinforcement theory.

Although structure is important for understanding language, it should be acknowledged that structure operates in the service of function. That is, the semantic, syntactic, and phonological structures of messages are consciously invoked for the purpose of making intent (function) recognizable. This is exceedingly important simply because special education, as evidenced by various language tests, has taken a structuralistic stance to the virtual exclusion of language functions. To that extent, special education has become disconnected from the scholarly literature.

> *Structure operates in the service of function.*

Special education has also become disconnected from the scholarly literature through its reliance on various psychometric normative tests of language. Most of these tests are problematical on several grounds:

a. They lack objectivity.

b. They lack construct validity.

c. They lack necessary and sufficient evidence.

> *Psychometric tests in special education may lack objectivity, construct validity, and necessary and sufficient evidence.*

Philosophers have shown that all human endeavors are inherently subjective, psychometric norms notwithstanding (Lakoff, 1987). Tests are subjective in their development (going in) and in their use (coming out). It is simply a popular myth that tests provide objective evidence.

Muma and Brannon (1986) reviewed the ten most widely used language tests in speech-language pathology. They found that none had construct validity as defined from a theoretical perspective (Messick, 1980, 1989, 1995). Moreover, a recent review of about twenty of the most widely used language tests again revealed a lack of construct validity (Muma, forthcoming). Although most language tests claimed to have construct validity, they did so based on the archaic "Holy Trinity for psychometric salvation" (Guion, 1977; Messick, 1980), whereby they utilized factor analysis, discriminate analysis, and trait analysis to claim construct validity. However, the test and measurement literature shifted away from these practices because construct validity needs to be established from theoretical perspectives in

> *Most tests do not meet the new standards for construct validity.*

order to ensure appropriate interpretations of the data (Messick, 1980, 1989, 1995).

Tests do not provide prima facie evidence of what an individual can do with language in actual social commerce. They merely provide elicited verbal performances that need to be extrapolated to what an individual might do in actual social commerce. Unfortunately, such performances are stripped of essential properties for drawing inferences as to what an individual can do in actual social commerce. Such performances are stripped of intent, context, repertoire, progress in acquisition sequences, strategies of learning, and active loci of learning. Furthermore, test performances convert language assessments to the misguided (Brown, 1973) efforts to ascertain rates of learning (grade-level, age-level, percentile rank) rather than sequences and repertoire. Over the past two decades the scholarly literature has shifted away from such measures to ascertain what an individual could do in actual social commerce (Muma, 1998). In doing so, the crucial assessment issues have become an individual's repertoire (semantic, syntactic, phonological, pragmatic), progress in acquisition sequences, strategies of learning, and active loci of learning. Unfortunately, special education has been silent about these issues.

> *The language tests do not provide prima facie evidence of what an individual can do in actual social commerce.*

Heterogeneity

Homogeneity is an implicit assumption of special education as evidenced by its reliance on normative tests, checklists, and structured programs. However, clinical populations are notoriously heterogeneous. It is impossible to find two or more individuals in any special education group who are precisely alike. Indeed, Baumeister (1984) indicated that the most outstanding characteristic of mental retardation is heterogeneity.

> *Clinical populations are notoriously heterogeneous.*

Special education in general, and deaf education in particular, need to be reoriented on the heterogeneous nature of individuals they serve. The various a priori practices have, in effect, made individuals conform to the service delivery practices rather than meet the needs of each individual.

None of the a priori efforts strive to ascertain what an individual can do in actual social commerce. The extent to which special education and deaf education rely on concepts and practices with the implicit homogeneity assumption is the extent to which these fields will be haunted to the core by the heterogeneous nature of special education populations (Muma, 1986, 1998). Indeed, such practices essentially ignore what an individual can do in actual social commerce and force, either directly or tacitly, comparisons to norms. By doing so, special education has adopted an implicit policy of abrogating individual skills or abilities.

> *Heterogeneity will haunt the clinical fields to the core.*

Technology: New Vistas or Packages

Technology has become a driving force in modern society. It has great potential for advancing special education. There are, of course, pros and cons in this arena. One of the contributions of technology is that it opens the door to many new vistas. By doing so, deaf education can become more aligned to the scholarly literature, thereby holding the potential for proactive stances.

On the other hand, technology can be misused to the extent that various substantive issues could be bypassed or misrepresented merely by clever packaging. Special education has already evidenced the misuse of technology by virtue of peddling assessment policies vested on tests lacking construct validity from a theoretical perspective. It has also pushed the evaluation button in the direction of gathering much data that is open to any interpretation thereby yielding data rather than evidence.

> *Technology can be helpful and also misused.*

Hopefully, technology and scholarship will unite in a constructive effort to move these professions forward. To that end, both have much to offer.

———≫·o·≪———

The field of deaf education needs to be theory-oriented simply because theories provide understandings. The crucial question becomes: Which scholarly views and perspectives underwrite deaf education? Speech act, relevance, and bootstrapping theories have been identified as among the most influential theories of language acquisition over the previous three decades. Neither the reinforcement theory nor the modality theory has been regarded as providing viable accounts of language acquisition.

When professional fields lack theoretical grounding, they become vulnerable to authoritarianship, dogma, hype, impressionism, and mis-used eclecticism. The crucial feature that threatens the scholarly stance of a profession is capriciousness. Eight issues in deaf education were identi-fied that raise questions about the level of scholarship in deaf education.

———≫·o·≪———

— Chapter 2 —
Why Deaf Education Needs to Be Theory-Oriented

John Muma, Ph.D., and Hank Teller, Ed.D.
University of Southern Mississippi

Need

In talking with many individuals in deaf education, both educators and teachers in the field, a prevailing attitude is the dismissal of theories in favor of the practical issues. This attitude could be expressed in the following way: "Don't give me theory; I want to know practical or 'hands-on' things to do." This attitude reveals a fundamental problem—that deaf education may be more interested in *how* to carry out various services than in understanding *why* particular services are appropriate.

> Some professionals do not want to deal with theories.

The irony, of course, is that the main purpose of theories is to provide appropriate understandings and, by doing so, making the substantive aspects of a theory practical. Thus, the prevailing attitude in deaf education reveals a serious misunderstanding about the main role of theories and a cleavage that separates deaf education from the appropriate scholarly literature simply because the scholarly literature is theory-driven.

> Theories make things practical.

The purpose of this chapter is to encourage a shift in perspective, whereby deaf education would strive to become theory-oriented toward a fuller understanding of more appropriate services. Indeed, a combination of relevant philosophical views and theoretical perspectives would go a long way toward justifiable rationales for *why* particular services are deemed appropriate. Appendix A provides a summary of several widely known and accepted philosophical views and theoretical perspectives.

What Philosophical Views Do

The purpose of philosophical views is to provide appropriate frames of reference or points of view from which theoretical perspectives may be posited. Philosophical views are evaluated in accordance with the coherence criteria. Searle (1992), the foremost scholar in the philosophy of cognition and language, provided a critique of several philosophical views of cognition and language. The central issue was coherence, the degree to which a particular philosophical view holds a rationally sound view across the issues addressed by that view. Specifically, Searle considered the following philosophical views: behaviorism, mentalism, monism, dualism, materialism, functionalism, and constructionism. Constructionism was deemed more coherent than the others and behaviorism was found to be among the least coherent.

> *Constructionism is more coherent than other views.*

Muma (1983) compared behaviorism with constructionism (mentalism). He showed that behaviorism is an instructional approach whereby the clinician or teacher makes decisions about content, sequences, rate, and reinforcement, and then administers activities to an individual or group. Thus, in behaviorism, the learner is thought to be a passive learner waiting to be taught and the province of learning is considered to be a teacher's decisions about content, sequences, rate, and reinforcement.

> *Behaviorism lacks coherence.*

In contrast, constructionism recognizes the learning process as an active process vested in each individual. Thus, the province of learning is invested in the child rather than the teacher. Therefore, it becomes necessary to ascertain an individual's available repertoire, progress in acquisition sequences, strategies of learning, and active loci of learning for semantic, syntactic, phonological, and pragmatic domains extending to the experiential, social, and emotional bases of language (Muma, 1998). By doing so, issues of content, sequences, rate, and intent are the province of the learner rather than the teacher. It is the role of the teacher to *describe* what the learner can do in actual social commerce, and then *facilitate* acquisition by varying the twelve contexts (Nelson, 1985) that support language acquisition, expanding repertoires, replacing early skills with subsequent skills

> *In constructionism, the province of learning is vested in the learner.*

in acquisition sequences, and exploiting active loci of learning (Muma, 1978, 1981, 1983, 1986, 1998, 2000; Muma & Teller, 2001).

Bruner (1981, p. 172) commented, "Context is all." He appreciated the multidimensional nature of communicative con-

texts. Nelson (1985) delineated twelve different aspects of communicative contexts. They are the following:

> *Context is all.*

Objective Context
Physical context: Immediate context, object,
   action, and relations
Cultural context: Cultural values and customs
Social context: Social interactions
Activity context: Activities and events
Agenda context: Intents, purposes, goals of activities
Affective context: Expressive or emotional state
Communicative act context: Type of speech acts
Action context: Relevant gestures that convey messages
Specific linguistic context: Basic ideas entailed
   in messages, relational meanings

Subjective Context
Cognitive context: Possible worlds, situated mind
Schemas: Perceived spatial, temporal, or causal
   relations
Event representations: Sequences of intentional action

Needless to say, facilitation of language acquisition should strive to vary these contexts toward increased repertoires, progress in acquisition sequences, and the exploitation of active loci of learning (Muma, 1978, 1986, 1998).

What Theories Do

Ironically, theories do precisely what many who complain about theories think they do not do. This is revealing on two accounts. First, the purposes of theories are to provide predictions, explanations, and understandings (Kaplan, 1964; Bohannon & Bonvillian, 2001). Understandings are what make theories practical. If teachers strive to understand a

> *Theories provide understandings.*

particular domain and establish appropriate rationales for rendering services in particular ways, they are well served by turning to relevant theories for direction and understanding. Without doing so, teachers are left to misused eclecticism which is the bane of scholarship and theory simply because certain eclectic views are little more than capricious views.

Second, if teachers or clinicians claim expertise in language, it behooves them to follow the relevant scholarly literature. That literature is theory-driven. Thus, when teachers choose not to be theory-oriented, they are also revealing that they are not interested in scholarship. If such views are widespread, then a profession becomes indicted for its lack of scholarship.

> *The scholarly literature is theory-driven.*

Just as philosophical views are scrutinized, theories are scrutinized as well. The philosophy of science has established criteria for scrutinizing theories. There are three levels for scrutinizing theories: descriptive, explanatory, and empirical adequacies (Bohannon & Bonvillian, 2001; Chomsky, 1957). These were discussed in Chapter 1.

Perera (1994), the editor of the *Journal of Child Language*, identified the five most influential theories of language acquisition over the previous twenty-five years. Not incidentally, these theories have achieved relatively high levels of descriptive, explanatory, and empirical adequacies. She identified the following:

> *The five most influential theories over the past three decades*

1. Government binding theory (Chomsky, 1981, 1982), parameter setting theory (Atkinson, 1992), and their cousin, learnability theory (Pinker, 1984, 1988)
2. Modularity theory (Fodor, 1983)
3. Relevance theory (Sperber & Wilson, 1986) and its predecessor, speech acts theory (Grice, 1975; Searle, 1969)
4. Bootstrapping theory (Bruner, 1981; Gleitman, 1994; Pinker, 1984, 1987)
5. Connectionism (McClelland & Rumelhart, 1986)

The basic notion underlying government and binding theory, parameter setting theory, and learnability theory is that humans are innately wired to learn language in particular ways. Three compelling kinds of evidence support this perspective. First, languages around the world share universals or common features even though they may differ structurally. Second, the onset of language acquisition around the world is remarkably similar. Third, the kinds of language problems encountered by those who have difficulty learning language or have limited verbal repertoires are not only remarkably similar but are consistent with normal language acquisition (Leonard, 1987, 1989). Thus, this perspective is the most eloquent innatist account of language acquisition.

> *Humans are uniquely wired to learn language.*

The basic notion underlying modularity is that the brain is organized into modules of functions, each of which is encapsulated, thereby operating independently of other modules. This notion seems to have credence concerning the primary sensory and motor systems (Geschwind, 1965a, b). However, it becomes increasingly difficult to hold this position for general cognition (Bever, 1992), representation (Karmiloff-Smith, 1992; Mandler, 1983), or the coin-of-the-realm of mental processing (Muma, 1986, 1998).

> *Modularity may hold for the primary sensory and motor areas of the brain but not for general cognition.*

Relevance and speech acts theories have shifted the orientation of language away from the traditional modality view (expressive/receptive language; auditory/visual processing) and the structuralistic view (semantics, syntax, phonology) to a cognitive–social perspective in which language functions (both cognitive and communicative) have priority over structure. By doing so, intent has become the "irreducible nucleus" of language (Bruner, 1986; Searle, 1992). Deaf education should render services based on intentional uses of language rather than the traditional drill activities.

> *The irreducible nucleus of language is intent.*

The basic notion underlying bootstrapping theories is context. Thus, as a child may do relatively well in one aspect of language, phonology for example, that skill may support or bootstrap learning in another aspect—syntax, for example. This means that contexts play crucial roles

> *Central issue for bootstrapping theories—context*

in language acquisition. Educators of the deaf should strive to vary the twelve kinds of contexts underlying language acquisition (Nelson, 1985) as a means of advancing an individual's verbal skills.

The basic notion underlying connectionism is associations between different aspects of language. This approach strives to account for language acquisition by virtue of computer simulation. The basic problem with such endeavors is the willingness to attribute human characteristics (anthropomorphism) to computer simulations that are neither contextually relevant nor intentional. For example, this perspective has a willingness to attribute thinking or intelligence to a computer based on high volumes of rapid information processing.

> *Connectionism relies on computer simulation.*

Dangers of Atheoretical Positions

Professions with an atheoretical bent have some serious problems. One problem is that they become susceptible to fads that yield capricious practices. Another problem is that they could care less about scholarship; such attitudes result in brutism. Still another problem is that the capricious nature of their services results in serious questions about the creditability of a profession. In effect, professionals who disdain theoretical perspectives are similar to the old-time tonic peddlers (pretenders) who glibly used various terms such as cognition, memory, language, semantics, and pragmatics, but who did not have the appropriate substantive knowledge for these issues. The following quote concerning cognition in adolescents as contrasted to that of preschoolers gives indirect homage to the importance of theories while indicting lay people, educators, and some psychologists for their failure to be theory-oriented: "Most lay people, most educators, and, in their nontheoretical modes, most developmental psychologists would not hesitate to answer affirmatively" (Nelson, 1996, p. 80). Thus, the implicit message is that most laymen, educators, and atheoretical developmental psychologists neither understand nor appreciate theoretical perspectives. Yet, it is precisely those perspectives that provide appropriate understandings and thereby advance a profession.

> *Professions that are atheoretical have serious problems.*

Brutism is merely imposing views and practices without substantive justification. Perhaps it is appropriate to turn to the Bible (Proverbs 12:1): "Whoso loveth instruction loveth knowledge; but he that hateth reproof *is* brutish." Dogma and eclecticism are mere stepdaughters of brutism simply because they are capricious.

> *Brutism imposes views and practices without appropriate evidence.*

When fundamental questions arise about the substantive nature of a profession, it becomes necessary to pause and reconsider the substantive nature from a theoretical perspective. Consider the following questions that continue to haunt special education in general, and speech-language pathology, learning disabilities, and deaf education in particular, even though several were raised many years ago:

a. **Theories of learning.** Cruickshank (1972) raised a central issue for the field of learning disabilities: What theoretical perspectives of learning comprise the substantive base of the field? It turns out that this field continues to be essentially atheoretical, with reliance placed on notions that issue from authoritarian stances such as the use of test norms that lack theoretical justification. Unfortunately, such stances are rampant across special education, resulting in political rather than scholarly positions.

> *The field of learning disabilities lacks a substantive base that deals with theories of learning.*

b. **Ecologically valid evidence.** Bronfenbrenner (1974, 1979) and Donaldson (1978) raised a fundamentally important issue for special education—the importance of ecologically valid evidence. Bronfenbrenner pointed out that children are asked to perform on research tasks (and we could include formal tests) in which they have never performed before and will never do again; yet, their performances are used to make judgments about how they will perform in the real world. Such rationalizing yields data that are ecologically invalid.

> *Professions that deal with people need ecologically based information.*

Donaldson showed that infants who did not evidence object permanence on the formal Uzgiris and Hunt (1975) test but where naming did evidence object permanence for "human sense" tasks that were ecologically appropriate. For example, these infants would reliably point to the kitchen when asked, "Where is Mommy?" when she was not present but in the kitchen. Brown (1986) underscored the importance of ecologically based evidence when he indicated that a study conducted in an actual social commerce is "more germane than all the laboratory studies" (p. 278).

c. **Lethal label.** The *Harvard Educational Review* published three special issues: (1) *Challenging the Myths: The Schools, the Blacks, and*

> *Education imposes lethal labels.*

the Poor (1971); (2) *The Rights of Children* (Part 1) (1973); and (3) *The Rights of Children* (Part 2) (1974). These issues raised fundamental questions concerning assessments in the schools. They indicated that schools use assessments to label children for eligibility for special education services, but these assessments typically lacked validity and failed to ascertain the nature of a problem. Once children become labeled, the educational system evidences reluctance to give up the labels when it should. This is precisely what Mercer (1972, 1974) called the "Lethal Label" problem in education.

Furthermore, the act of labeling raises the prospect of the nominalist fallacy. This fallacy occurs when someone thinks that

> *Beware of the subtle dangers of the nominalist fallacy.*

". . . giving a phenomenon a special name sufficiently explains the phenomenon" (Bohannon & Bonvillian, 2001, p. 299). This fallacy arises because the various language tests do not provide necessary and sufficient information to describe the nature of a problem (Muma, 1998). It is necessary to describe an individual's available repertoire (Ninio, Snow, Pan, & Rollins, 1994), progress in acquisition sequences (Brown, 1973), and active loci of learning (Bloom, Hood, & Lightbown, 1974; Muma, 1983, 1986, 1998) in order to under stand the nature of a problem.

d. **Language sampling**: In a survey of over ninety studies that employed language sampling, Muma and Brannon (1986) found that the prevailing practices were the reliances on 50- or 100-utterance language samples. For example, Lee (1974), Lee and

Canter (1971), Miller and Chapman (1981), and Watkins and Rice (1991) used 50-utterance samples, and Tyack and Gottsleben (1977) used 100-utterance samples to assess presumed language skills. "Many have suggested 50 to 100 different utterances as a sample for clinical analysis" (Lahey, 1988, p. 294). "For efficient yet valid clinical data gathering, then, a 50-utterance sample is usually adequate" (Paul, 1995, p. 300). Miller (2001, p. 5) indicated that 25 utterances "provide the same information as longer samples on many variables. . . ." Yet, Brown (1973) and Lahey (1988) indicated that language samples for grammatical assessment should be at least 200 utterances. Thus, a paradox arises concerning language sample size for grammatical assessment. The paradox is the difference between the prevailing practices in special education of 50 or 100 utterances and the recommended sample sizes of at least 200 utterances by the scholars.

> *The prevailing language sampling practices in special education are the uses of 50- or 100-utterances.*

Muma, Morales, Day, Tackett, Smith, Daniel, Logue, and Morriss (1998) studied the sampling error rates for 50-, 100-, 200-, and 400-utterance language samples. They found that 50-, 100-, and 200- utterance samples have the following respective error rates when compared to 400-utterance samples: 55%, 40%, and 15%. Needless to say, the prevailing language sample sizes of 50 or 100 utterances in speech-language pathology have excessive error rates.

> *The language sampling error rates are excessive for 50- and 100-utterance samples.*

e. **Specific language impairment (SLI):** The traditional ways to deal with language impairment have been in terms of language delay and/or language deviance. However, Leonard (1987, 1989) showed that language problems were neither delayed nor deviant but rather evidenced "specific language impairment (SLI)" (1987, p. 1). Stark and Tallal (1981) and Plante (1998) attempted to

> *Specific language impairment has been linked to CA, MA, and LA.*

formalize the SLI notion with regard to chronological age (CA), mental age (MA), and language age (LA). Such ventures reflect an allegiance to formal experimentation at the cost of ignoring ecologically valid evidence, most notably repertoire, progress in acquisition sequences, and active loci of learning.

Tager-Flusberg and Cooper (1999) attempted to further solidify the notion of specific language impairment by imposing a normative perspective by virtue of striving for a phenotype. Unfortunately, such endeavors have a fundamental flaw: the normative perspective has the underlying assumption of homogeneity, whereas clinical populations are notoriously heterogeneous. Muma (1991) showed that Leonard's (1987, 1989) attempts to substantiate SLI in terms of "low phonetic substance" following Pinker's (1984) learnability theory was doomed from the outset simply because it is based on the underlying homogeneity assumption. Indeed, Leonard indicated that individual differences hindered his attempt to show that individuals who have SLI problems had "low phonetic substance" difficulties. Muma et al. (1998) showed that the core notion for grammatical skills greatly misrepresents repertoires for normal children. Inasmuch as clinical populations are much more heterogeneous than normal populations, the notion of a core problem for SLI is misguided. Rather, more appropriate ways to address the heterogeneous nature of clinical populations are in terms of repertoire, progress in acquisition sequences, alternative learning strategies, and active loci of learning. Thus, the SLI notion should be construed whereby *specific* is regarded as the product of *specifying* the nature of an individual's language impairment.

> *SLI has been defined from the homogeneity assumption.*

> *If SLI were defined with the heterogeneity assumption, specific would be regarded as the product of specifying an individual's repertoire, progress in acquisition sequences, strategies, and active loci of learning.*

f. **Diagnosis:** Strangely, speech-language pathology has adopted the medical term of *diagnostics* to refer to various clinical assessment procedures in language (cognition, semantics, syntax, phonology, pragmatics, socialization). The dictionary defines *diagnosis* as (1) the art or act of recognizing disease from its symptoms; also, the decision reached; and (2) scientific determination; critical scrutiny or its resulting judgment.

> *Rather than diagnosis, the clinical fields deal with assessment.*

As for the first issue, it would be a stretch to believe that the kinds of language assessments constitute evidence for recognizing disease from its symptoms. For instance, problems with articulation provide evidence of speech problems, but should such problems be considered symptomatic of a disease or the decision reached? In addition, the notion of symptomology implicates causal relations. Except for causal issues such as hearing loss, the causes of most speech and language problems are essentially speculative and beyond assessment.

As for the second issue, the extent to which the assessment process is construct based (Messick, 1980, 1989, 1995) is the extent to which a scientific determination is made or critical scrutiny is performed. Thus, the second issue holds some justification for regarding the assessment of speech and language problems as a diagnosis. However, closer scrutiny of the speech and language tests (Muma, 1998, forthcoming; Muma & Brannon, 1986) raises serious questions about whether such assessments have construct validity. Indeed, Huang, Hopkins, and Nippold (1998) showed that about half of the speech-language pathology clinicians in the field are dissatisfied with these tests presumably because of their lack of construct validity. Under these circumstances, the act of rendering language assessments fails to meet the criteria for diagnosis even though the field of speech-language pathology claims to render "diagnostics."

Borrowing

> *"Borrowing" can regarded as symptomatic of a lack of integrity and scholarship.*

Atheoretical professions are at risk for ethical infractions. For example, "borrowing" (a polite term for plagiarism) is symptomatic of atheoretical professions. Such activities may have occurred in special education. Here are a few examples that might be construed as this kind of borrowing:

   a. Renfrew (1966) identified and described eleven steps toward overcoming the open syllable. Yet, some others have merely renamed the open syllable as "final consonant deletion" (Hodson, 1986). Vygotsky (1962) described scientific and spontaneous word learning. Spontaneous word learning occurs when a child has an experiential base of knowledge that affords him or her at least a rudimentary understanding of something that is named, whereupon that name becomes known. This notion of spontaneously knowing the meaning of words has been renamed as "fast mapping" (Rice, Buhr, & Nemeth, 1990).

   b. Muma (1978, 1983) described the role of a clinician as providing selective language models in actual social commerce. Yet, the notion of "focused stimulation" appears to be remarkably similar (Fey, 1986). However, Muma (1998) attempted to distance "focused stimulation" from the "parallel talk strategy" by indicating that the former is behavioristic in nature and the latter is constructionistic. Thus, their underlying philosophical views and their attendant practices are conceptually different.

   c. Expansions (Brown & Bellugi, 1963) and expatiations (Cazden, 1965; McNeill, 1966) are two of ten language intervention techniques (Muma, 1971), and communicative payoff (Muma, 1981) is another intervention approach. These are remarkably similar to Ratner's (2001, p. 380) comments about expansions, recasting, and scaffolding. Except for the behavioristic notion of fading, the latter is also similar to Bruner's (1981) notion of scaffolding.

There are other instances of borrowing in special education but there is no need to pursue this topic here except to say that it is symptomatic of atheoretical and unscientific professions.

Atheoretical Signatures

The characteristics of atheoretical professions include both operationalism and emotionalism. Operationalism is evidenced by having things to do regardless of the values of the activities. It is common in special education to operate with a variety of check-lists of dubious value. Cazden (1972) cautioned that to merely become operational does not assure valid nor appropriate services. For example, some professionals have used elaborate checklists that presumably assess a child's language abilities, but the question arises as to

> *Making teachers operational is not the same as providing appropriate education.*

whether such checklists provide valid evidence of what a child can do with language in actual social commerce. Muma (1986) raised several questions about the validity of such checklists.

Another characteristic of atheoretical professions is a reversion to emotions. Scholarship rests on inquiry. However, a clear indication of a lack of an appreciation of scholarship is when people become

> *Scholarship rests on inquiry rather than emotion.*

emotional rather than address substantive issues. Such people operate outside of theoretical perspectives and evidence unscholarly conduct.

Summary

Philosophical views and theoretical perspectives comprise the substantive base of a scholarly profession because they provide appropriate and disciplined understandings. Professional fields that disdain such views and perspectives become political, and their substantive issues revert to nothing more than authoritarianism, dogma, and hype. ". . . Sound clinical practice should be based, in large part, on the relevant basic and applied research rather than pronouncements by authorities, intuition, or dogma" (Schiavetti & Metz, 1997, p. 3).

———⟫‣0‣⟪———

Cognitive socialization offers deaf education many new princi-
ples and practices toward more appropriate educational services for the
deaf and hard of hearing. Several different theoretical perspectives with-
in cognitive socialization are considered. Langer's views are especially
interesting because they focus on several myths in education.

———⟫‣0‣⟪———

— Chapter 3 —

Cognitive Socialization: Implications for the Classroom

Sharon Baker, Ed.D.
University of Tulsa

Rote memorization has played a significant role in the education of students who are deaf or hard of hearing, regardless of the communication philosophy of the school. Early writings that describe classrooms for students who are deaf or hard of hearing often advocated instructional techniques that relied extensively on rote memorization and drill of language structures. During the 1800s, the National Institute for the Deaf in Paris held public exhibitions of students' abilities to analyze grammar, recite passages, or explain philosophical questions in which they had been previously drilled (Lane, 1989). The measure of learning depended greatly on one's ability to memorize; therefore, those who memorized well were deemed more successful than others. Instructional techniques in both oral and manual classrooms relied extensively on drill and repetition to teach content as well as discrete grammatical structures of language to their students. This practice continued until the 1950s when natural approaches were introduced to the field (Groht, 1958; McAnally, Rose, & Quigley, 1994).

> *Many traditional views and practices remain, even though the literature has changed.*

As with many aspects of education, instructional philosophies tend to be cyclical, and much of what happens in regular education eventually influences deaf education. Recently, instructional philosophies reflecting more holistic and constructionistic approaches to learning have replaced memorization and drill. The field of deaf education gained much from the philosophies of whole language and literacy-based instruction (Schleper, 1995) and balanced approaches to literacy (Schirmer, 2000).

However, current educational programs belie a trend in regular education to return to traditional teaching strategies, notably drill and the

There is a tendency to revert back to some traditional views and practices.

memorization of isolated facts unrelated to the lives children experience. With increased requirements for all schools to follow state standards and use state-adopted textbooks, and with the increased participation of deaf and hard of hearing students in state-mandated testing programs, much of what teachers do currently, regardless of where they teach, is driven by educational reform and accountability.

The focus on accountability during the 1990s, through federal and

Accountability may have intruded in deleterious ways.

state policies, has elevated the role that standardized testing plays in schools and programs in the U.S., and as a consequence, teachers are changing not only *what* they teach in order to follow state standards or core competencies, but also *how* they teach in

response to these requirements.

While the state and national directives related to educational accountability leave schools and teachers with little discretion, it must be understood that the present trend is antithetical to what we know about language development. The central questions that we must investigate are:

a. Is there evidence that student learning is improved because of increased accountability and testing, that is, do outcomes provide evidence that appropriate learning is occurring?

b. How will deaf and hard of hearing students acquire useful language skills under these teaching conditions, especially in view of the fact that the scholarly literature has shifted away from structure in favor of function, notably the centrality of intent (Bruner, 1986; Muma, 1986, 1998; Nelson, 1985, 1986, 1996; Searle, 1992)? Standardized testing and accountability may have actually created a cleavage between what the literature in cognition and language acquisition has to offer and what is implicated by test scores, and so on.

c. Should teachers resort to drill and repetitive practices in order to prepare students to take tests, or are there alternative theories and instructional methods that may facilitate learning in more meaningful and productive ways?

With these questions in mind, it becomes necessary to consider theories that have influenced teaching and learning and new theories that can be applied to classrooms for students who are deaf or hard of hearing.

Theoretical Perspectives

For several decades behavioral theories of stimulus-response with the goal of prediction and control of behavior have played a major role in the IEP-driven educational process for children who are deaf or hard of hearing (e.g., observable objective; stimulus; behavior/response; reinforcement/reward). Behavioral theorists place values on the environment from which they believed learning transpires. They think that children are passive learners; that learning is dispensed by teachers who presumably control content, sequencing, pacing, and reinforcement (Muma, 1983); and that learning presumably occurs as a function of rewards and reinforcement. Although behaviorism and reinforcement theory have defined the dominant classroom practices in schools, other philosophical views and theoretical perspectives are beginning to change the educational landscape because the developments in the scholarly literature have much to offer toward improved services in deaf education.

> *Stimulus-response education has become challenged.*

Unfortunately, behaviorism and reinforcement theory were found to be seriously flawed in regard to coherence and descriptive and explanatory adequacies of theories. Consequently, reinforcement theory has been dismissed as a viable account of language acquisition. Bruner (1978) indicated that ". . . the new approach to language has sparked a revolt against traditional 'cause-effect' psychology and raised deep questions about the adequacy of positivist theories. A central element in the revolt is the contrast between 'caused' and 'intended' behaviour" (p. viii). He indicated that the positivist notions (reinforcement theory) were "corrosive dogma" because they lacked appropriate descriptive and explanatory evidence and because they were open to virtually any interpretation. "Models of language acquisition built

> *Reinforcement theory has not held up to scholarly scrutiny.*

explicitly on assumptions of positive and negative reinforcement are no longer acceptable" (Nelson, 1985, p. 33).

The cognitive socialization view is especially attractive because it offers approximately forty major advancements over previous notions concerning cognition and language acquisition. The cognitive socializa-

Cognitive socialization has continuity with constructionism and some viable theories of language acquisition.

tion view has continuity with constructionism and functionalism rather than behaviorism, reductionism, and quantification. Searle (1992) showed that constructionism, and to some extent functionalism, more fully meet the criterion of coherence than the other philosophical views. Furthermore, cognitive socialization is attractive because it has substantive continuity with the five most influential theories of language acquisition over the past three decades, as identified by the editor of the *Journal of Child Language* (Perera, 1994).

The constructive nature of cognitive socialization recognizes that active cognition underlies language acquisition with its experiential-

Cognitive socialization has continuity with an individual's experiential, social, cultural, and emotional bases of learning.

social-emotional-cultural influences (Bruner, 1986, 1990; Muma, 1986, 1998; Nelson, 1985, 1986, 1996). Mandler (1979) indicated that "cognitive growth occurs mainly in a social nexus" (p. 375). Furthermore, this orientation holds that intent is the essence of language, indeed cognition. Bruner (1986) and Searle (1992) indicated that intent is the irreducible nucleus of language acquisition and use. Brown (1973) showed that rate of learning indices such as age or grade levels are notoriously varied whereas sequence is highly stable. This means that it is necessary to assess what an individual can do with language in terms of progress in acquisition sequences, available repertoires, and active loci of learning rather than age level, grade level, or percentile rank.

Cognitive socialization has continuity with speech acts, relevance, and bootstrapping theories.

With the developments of speech acts (Clark & Clark, 1977), relevance (Sperber & Wilson, 1986), and bootstrapping theories (Gleitman, 1994; Pinker, 1984), it has become clear that language is much more than words and sentences. Rather, the structure of language serves the functions of language toward making intent recognizable. The two main cognitive functions of language are representation (Mandler, 1983) and mediation (Nelson, 1996); and the two main communicative functions of language are intent (Bruner, 1986; Searle, 1992) and content (Sperber & Wilson, 1986), with the latter being composed of explicit content (basic ideas entailed in messages) and implicit content (possible worlds, situated minds, knowledge of the world) that makes explicit content comprehensible.

Spontaneous language (speech or signed) constitutes prima facia evidence of what an individual can do in actual social commerce (Muma, 1986, 1998). In contrast, elicited verbal behavior is selective, constrained, and unrepresentative of what an individual can do. There is somewhat of a paradox in education whereby claims are made about children's presumed language abilities based on elicited verbal behavior; yet, it is what an individual *does* in actual social commerce that provides appropriate evidence of what that individual *can* do. Elicited behavior occurs in structured educational activities, in test performances, and, even worse, as secondhand impressions on checklists.

> *Spontaneous language samples provide prima facie evidence of what an individual can do with language.*

For language to be acquired through social interaction requires those who are communicating to have a shared language in order to operate on "mutual manifestness" (Sperber & Wilson, 1986). There is a question as to what extent deaf children have an experiential-social-cognitive-cultural base that is sufficiently comparable within the Deaf community and between that community and the hearing community to render appropriate communication.

> *Social interaction is crucial for language acquisition.*

Meier (1991) stated that many deaf children with hearing parents experience relatively little child-directed speech or signed language in early childhood. According to Pelley (2000), Shepard-Kegl, a linguist documenting the emergence of sign language in Nicaragua, researched deaf children in isolated, rural communities where communication was limited to a homesign system. She found that these children failed to develop a functional language system, thus implicating cognitive socialization theories. For Kegl, language is in the brain, but in order for language to develop there has to be "a fuel" and that fuel is communication (Pelley, 2000) in actual social commerce (Muma, 1986, 1998).

Cognitive socialization also draws from constructivism which states that knowledge is constructed within the individual and that development is not governed by external teachings as believed by behaviorists.

Cognitive socialization pertains to an individual who is an active processor of information.

Instead, development is an active process of construction in which children, through their own interaction with others, build increasingly differentiated and comprehensive cognitive structures (Crain, 1992; Mandler, 1983). Early constructivists including Piaget (1955) did not believe that children's thinking was shaped by adult teachings or other contrived environmental influences. Piaget believed that children must interact with the environment to develop, but it is they, not the external environment, who build new cognitive structures.

Constructionist teachers facilitate learning rather than instruct.

Constructivist teachers view themselves as facilitators of learning who arrange experiences and initiate situations that allow children to develop language through genuine interest and interaction with others. Rote memorization, isolated from relevant application, is viewed as a waste of educational time because information that is memorized is most often stored initially in short-term memory, and if the information is not applied or deemed necessary to the student in a relevant and meaningful way, the information rapidly decays.

Memory is not an entity that can be isolated from an individual's repertoire.

In cognitive socialization, cognition refers to how the mind works, including its ability to categorize, represent, attend, plan, and execute tasks. Memory is a key component of cognition. Recent research in the areas of neuroscience has brought greater insights into memory, brain development, human learning, and how these affect language acquisition. One development is that memory is no longer considered to be an entity that can be isolated from a skill in which memory functions (Hudson & Fivush, 1990).

Langer's Perspectives

Langer (1997), a professor of psychology at Harvard University, offered the **cognitive deterioration** perspective concerning cognition in the elderly. Langer examined attitudes toward aging in two cultures: the American Deaf and the mainland Chinese cultures. The results of her research were that the "elder Deaf and elder Chinese participants clearly outperformed the elder hearing, non-Chinese groups" in terms of memory skills and that negative views toward aging correlated with poorer performance in the older groups (p. 97). This research supports the view that cultural beliefs about aging play a role in determining the degree of memory loss experienced in old age.

How does this relate to deaf and hard of hearing students? Langer concluded that rigid mindsets about ourselves affect performance. Children who seem not to care about school may have created rigid mindsets because of negative assessments of their abilities (i.e., self-fulfilling prophecies).

> *Rigid mindsets may be deleterious for learning.*

Since cultural attitudes play a powerful role in cognition and memory, this has implications for the instruction of deaf and hard of hearing students. First, rigid [negative] mindsets affect performance; therefore, teacher expectations may influence student achievement. Low expectations have been linked to the lack of academic achievement (Johnson, Liddell, & Erting, 1989). Part of this social dilemma may have to do with long-standing stereotypes and negative labels by the majority culture that describe deaf people as incapable of doing for them-selves. Fortunately these stereotypes are vanishing, partly as a result of the cultural revolution that occurred in the 1980s (Lane, Hoffmeister, & Behan, 1996). This revolution brought about cultural aware-ness and linguistic change in the field of deaf educa-tion. However, there are still deaf educators who

> *Stereotypes concerning the deaf and hard of hearing may be operating in the non-deaf population.*

believe that deaf and hard of hearing students are incapable of achieving educational parity. Second, paternalism (Lane, 1992), the notion that we must protect deaf people and do for them because they are vulnerable and unable to do for themselves, leads to a state of learned helplessness. Both low expectations and learned helplessness affect how children learn and impact on student outcomes.

In addition to theories of cognitive deterioration, Langer proposed the theory of **mindful learning** that may bring additional insights into the nature of learning and memory, as components of cognitive

Mindful learning refers to one's awareness and openness for learning.	socialization become applied to the education of students who are deaf or hard of hearing. Mindful learning refers to an openness and awareness of one's own learning process. Langer identified seven pervasive mindsets that undermine the process of learning and how to avoid their debilitating effects.

These are discussed below.

Mindful Learning.

A mindful approach to any activity has three characteristics: the continuous creation of new categories; openness to new information; and an implicit awareness of more than one perspective. Mindlessness, in contrast, is characterized by an entrapment in old categories; by automatic behavior that precludes attending to new signals; and by action that operates from a single perspective. Being mindless is like being on automatic pilot. (Langer, 1997, p. 4)

Several myths in education hinder mindful learning.

Sadly, much of what passes for learning in schools is actually the rote, mindless passing of time. The following are myths of instruction that Langer says promote mindless learning:

Myth 1. The basics must be learned so well that they become second nature. Learning the basics means rote memorization of high stakes test-driven facts. However, Langer (1997) commented, "Learning the basics in a rote, unthinking manner almost ensures mediocrity" (p. 14). At the least, it deprives learners of maximizing their own potential for more effective performance and enjoyment of learning. "The key to this new way of teaching is based on an appreciation of both the conditional, context-dependent nature of the world and the value of uncertainty" (p. 15). Langer suggested that content should be taught conditionally (i.e., this could be a *weapon*). The more students learn from the start that there are different ways of looking at the information (i.e., different perspectives), the more creative thinking becomes. Rather than learning

Sideways learning: a student's awareness that issues can be considered from a variety of perspectives.

information directly, Langer proposed an approach called **sideways learning**. Sideways learning aims at maintaining a mindful state. Mindfulness revolves around certain psychological states by creating (p. 23):

- openness to novelty
- alertness to distinction
- sensitivity to different contexts
- implicit, if not explicit, awareness of multiple perspectives
- orientation in the present. Each leads back to the other and back to itself.

Myth 2. **Paying attention means staying focused on one thing at a time.** From early childhood, students are taught that paying attention means being still and focusing only on the matter at hand. If focus wanders, the child is said to be distracted, but when students are distracted they are paying attention to something else. Rather than wondering why a student became distracted, educators should consider what is so attractive about the alternative stimuli. Teachers usually believe that if students fix their minds on the work they will learn,

> *Forced attention may be at the cost of other learning.*

but the mind naturally seeks variety as stated by the discrepancy learning theory (Kagan, 1970; Kagan & Lewis, 1965). "In order to pay attention to something for any amount of time the image must be varied. To pay constant, fixed attention to a thought or an image may be a kind of oxymoron" (Langer, 1997, p. 39).

For example, Langer (1997) studied adults as they read short stories. The mindful groups were instructed to vary aspects of each story as they read it (i.e., to read the text from different perspectives, to consider different endings, and so on). The mindless groups were told to focus on specific aspects of each story. The people who had been asked to vary what they read, those in the mindful groups, remembered significantly more details than did members of the other groups. Interestingly, the mindful groups had more to think about and they remembered more. Varying the target of our attention, whether an object or an idea, evidently improves our recall of it.

Langer (1997) suggested:

The most effective way to increase our ability to pay attention is
to look for the novelty within the stimulus situation, whether it is a story, a map, or a painting.
This is the most useful lesson to teach children,
because it enables them to be relatively independent of other people and of their physical
environment. (p. 43)

> *Novel stimuli may lead to more flexible and dynamic learning.*

Paying attention to stilted information is boring and draining. In
contrast, paying attention to novel stimuli is energizing and allows one
to sustain attention for long periods of time.

> *Discrepancy learning has effectively kept the students' attention.*

Sesame Street incorporated discrepancy learning
theory; i.e., "This program is brought to you by the
number four" (four of many different items were
presented). Children who were claimed to have
short attention spans were either "glued" to the TV
or evidenced "dual processing."

Classroom discussions that encourage students to vary the target of
attention and to look at the novelty of the situation or story may
increase memory and learning. These discussions, which allow students
to interact with others, are congruent with cognitive socialization. In
addition, spontaneous conversation is inherently novel and should be
incorporated in education, especially in peer interactions.

Myth 3. Delaying gratification is important. Rewards are commonly

> *Providing rewards detracts from appreciating the inherent value of learning.*

used in schools. Students are provided with increasingly more enticing trinkets in exchange for doing
their work and not interrupting the work of others.
This kind of system, based on the behavioral theories
of stimulus-response, teaches children nothing about
the inherent value of learning.

Another reward practice is to remind children that what they are
doing will help them in the future. They are told that our instruction will
be important in the future, when they grow up. Try convincing an ado-
lescent who is contemplating gang membership that differentiating
between present tense and perfect tense is important to his future. He is

much more interested in coping with his feelings of powerlessness, self-doubt, and loneliness than in passing an English test.

Mindful engagement in learning involves the enjoyment that students receive from the process of learning, that is, going from not knowing to knowing. The rewards are intrinsic and immediate. Role-playing a scenario in which he uses the perfect tense ("I've had it with you") to stand down a bully is immediately and intrinsically rewarding, is much more relevant to the student, and is motivated by his intent, which is the essence of language.

> *Enjoyment of learning is sufficient in and of itself.*

Myth 4. Rote memorization is necessary in education. According to Langer (1997), "memorizing is a strategy for taking in material that has no personal meaning" (p. 68). Higher levels of student boredom occur in schools that emphasize memorization and drills (MacIver & Epstein, 1994). "Memorization appears to be inefficient for long-term retention of information, and it is usually undertaken for purposes of evaluation by others" (Langer, p. 72). Memorization is difficult and rarely fun. When providing language instruction (e.g., English), the goal should be to understand while learning practical applications rather than memorization of grammar rules. What teachers of deaf and hard of hearing students should strive for is to help students understand that there are contextual factors that influence perception. "If we simply memorize the known past, we are not preparing students for the future" (Langer, p. 82). Pragmatically based language activities are interactive, and interactive learning inherently is more appropriate than rote learning.

> *Memorization is of questionable value for education.*

Myth 5. Forgetting is a problem. Information may be remembered in two ways: mindlessly or mindfully. In mindless learning students accept information unconditionally or by memorizing it. Langer (1997) feels students may be better off forgetting these context-free facts because such facts tend to circumscribe learning. Forgetting allows students to arrive at better solutions that are based on experience and take into consideration the present context. Besides, one can always look facts up in a book. Problem-solving activities such as thinking of

> *Forgetting is expected when the information loses utility.*

the best way to ask for a date or the best way to ask for a raise in your allowance are more likely to improve vocabulary than memorizing a list of words.

Myth 6. Intelligence is knowing "what's out there." Intelligence to many theorists means knowing what is out there; however, the newer cognitive literature has dropped this notion and replaced it with experiential, social, emotional, and cultural views of reality as defined by the situated mind (Nelson, 1996) or possible worlds (Bruner, 1986). Mindful intelligence is the view that individuals may define their relation to their environment in several ways, essentially creating their own reality.

> *One's possible worlds or situated mind is the product of living in the world.*

Perceptions are relative to our past experiences (Garner, 1966) but experiences differ from person to person. Multiple perspectives help individuals to appreciate novelty in information. Langer (1997) said, "There is no absolute optimum standard for action. From a mindful perspective, one's stance on a particular situation is not an attempt to make the best choice from among the available options but to create options" (p. 114). Rather than look for external standards of optimal fit or the right answers, one discovers that the standard perpetually changes within the realm of experiences. This principle, too, is consistent with cognitive socialization in a pragmatically based language classroom. For example, memorizing a list of nouns and a list of verbs does not ensure that a child can put them together to make intent recognizable (Sperber & Wilson, 1986).

> *Perception is relative to one's knowledge of the world.*

Myth 7. There are right and wrong answers. Cognition is often seen as the capacity to achieve desirable outcomes, to get the right answer. Langer (1997) believes that when a person is mindful, that person realizes that every inadequate answer is adequate in another context. See the theory of natural categories (Rosch, 1973).

> *Answers are neither right nor wrong but conditional.*

In the perspective of every person lies a lens through which we may better understand ourselves. If we respect students' abilities to define their own experiences, to generate their own hypotheses, and to discover new ways of categorizing the world, we might not be so quick to evaluate the adequacy of their answers. We might, instead, begin listening to their questions. Out of the questions of students come some of the most creative ideas and discoveries. (Langer, 1997; p. 135)

The constructionist's view has provided new strategies to enhance learning and memory within the context of social interaction (Bruner, 1986; Langer, 1997; Rogoff, 1990; Vygotsky, 1962). How can the concepts presented by Langer apply to the classrooms for students who are deaf or hard of hearing? There are direct implications of these views for education of the deaf and hard of hearing.

Classrooms for Students Who Are Deaf or Hard of Hearing

It is difficult to describe a typical classroom because of the various configurations and types of schools that deaf and hard of hearing children attend. However, the following are examples of typical classroom structures and activities that will help provide a basis for considering and incorporating the distinctions between mindful and mindless learning.

Self-contained elementary and secondary classrooms often use traditional group instruction with students sitting in a semicircle and the teacher instructing the students on a particular topic. Careful observation of this classroom reveals that teachers spend a great deal of time trying to capture and control the students' attention. Teachers frequently sign/say PAY ATTENTION or WATCH ME. Sometimes they will flash the lights, stomp on the floor, or tap on the students' desks to get their attention. This effort to get all the students' eyes on the teacher at the same time in order to capture the instructional moment is difficult to achieve. The moment the teacher looks down or turns away to write on the board and visual contact is lost, students tend to engage in behaviors that have nothing to do

> *The traditional classroom typically lacks support for mindful learning.*

with what the teacher is teaching. They may have sideline discussions about topics of interest such as what will be served at lunch; they may make snippet comments to other students in order to get a charged reaction; they may make plans for the evening, and so on. As a consequence, much of the instructional period that is typically 50–60 minutes long is spent struggling to maintain joint attention so that learning will occur. Sometimes the teacher will divide up the class and work with a small group while the others work on individual assignments. Sometimes teachers will install study carrels for students who are highly distractible in an effort to isolate them from other students. This classroom exemplifies a behavioral approach where teachers are trying to maintain attention so that information can be transmitted into the minds of the students.

The next example of a classroom for deaf and hard of hearing students is quite different than the one just described and is frequently found in public schools. The teacher most often employs one-on-one teaching arrangements in order to address the diverse needs of the students. This particular approach is often defined as a resource classroom serving deaf and hard of hearing students who are mainstreamed into the regular classroom and return for part of the day to a deaf educator. Scheduling students into the resource room is challenging because of the heterogeneity of the students (e.g., a teacher could be responsible for three or four different grade levels). Even when students are mainstreamed, the resource room teacher usually tutors students in content areas and teaches the language-dependent classes. In resource rooms, language instruction typically involves students working individually on assignments because they are usually working on different subjects and at different grade levels. During language instruction, teachers often use prepared language programs that incorporate worksheets and workbooks in order to allow students to work independently. Students work individually on assignments because the teacher is serving multiple grade levels simultaneously and the students are functioning at different stages of language development. The packaged language programs are a convenient way to address the wide range of abilities and levels within the resource classroom; consequently, language instruction becomes more drill in structures, isolated from meaning, and the carryover to functional language

> *The constructionist classroom typically supports mindful learning.*

use is questionable. In this setting convenience or expedience may have replaced appropriateness and relevance, thereby defining the educational process to meet the needs of teachers rather than the needs of students.

Making this classroom more mindful is much more challenging in this academic setting because of scheduling and time constraints. However, if learning language requires social interaction, this type of classroom structure falls short since students rarely have the opportunity to interact with each other in meaningful, sustained dialogue. Having students complete worksheets and workbooks is mindless and contributes little to language learning.

Social interaction is expected in a classroom that supports mindful learning.

In order to facilitate language development and language growth in students who are deaf or hard of hearing, teachers of language must be aware of the differences between mindless and mindful learning, for much of what occurs in the classroom may not lead to advancements in communication and cognition (Sperber & Wilson, 1986).

Making the previously described classrooms more mindful requires that the teacher limit direct teaching and lecture, encourage discussion about topics that interest students, encourage students to use sideways learning, and identify elements of the topic or story that are novel or distinctive. Teachers should use instructional strategies that rely less on memorization of vocabulary and facts. Instead, students should use problem-solving skills to analyze topics and stories. Students should understand that the appropriate answer often depends on the context of the situation. Teachers

It is easy to identify teachers who support mindful learning.

should use conditional descriptions rather than absolutes and discuss the various possibilities or outcomes (Kagan, 1970). And last, students should be encouraged to investigate the multiple perspectives that exist because learning about the perspectives of others facilitates greater understanding of the issues (Vygotsky, 1962).

In addition to activities that promote mindful learning, the **project approach** to teaching may also provide students with opportunities to learn language through interactions with others. The project approach strives to engage students in activities that have relevance to their lives and in which they are

The project approach to teaching has continuity with mindful learning.

genuinely interested. It is an in-depth study of a particular topic. Typically projects in early childhood start by the students learning about themselves and their immediate family. From there learning becomes more abstract and remote but socially and culturally justified. By middle school, students are learning about national and world events; and by high school, students are engaging in projects that revolve around critical issues. The project approach takes into consideration the unevenness of students' development by planning for a wide range of activities at varying levels of complexity. Projects encourage students to work together and to collaborate in their learning. During the active learning stage, students discuss, investigate, inquire, interview experts, search for information and document their findings (e.g., students write articles, make videos and posters, and construct models that reflect what they have learned).

Even though schools must operate under the current policies and mandates related to accountability and students will be required to take standardized tests that will be used as evidence of learning, there are still many opportunities for learning that may increase the language skills and subsequent literacy abilities of children who are deaf or hard of hearing.

Many aspects of traditional, back-to-basics education fail to meet the educational challenges of children who are deaf or hard of hearing; therefore, taking a different approach is plausible. However, the more telling motivation for incorporating cognitive socialization is that it is aligned with major new developments in the scholarly literature and therefore holds good promise for advancing the field of deaf education. As the cognitive socialization becomes incorporated into education, the classrooms for students who are deaf or hard of hearing may indeed change from behavioral models where the teacher's main focus is on behavior and classroom control and where students are viewed as empty vessels into which language is poured, to classrooms where students are allowed the opportunity to learn and construct their own understandings through experiences and meaningful interactions with others with whom they share a common language. Much can be gained by incorporating the

> *Given the developments in the contemporary literature, teachers may want to shift away from the traditional reinforcement approach to the cognitive socialization approach.*

cognitive socialization approach toward viewing deaf or hard of hearing children as individuals capable of acquiring rich and complex language systems.

—————➤∘◀—————

The sociocultural approach to deaf education raises the question of distinctions between the traditional and constructivist approaches to education. By focusing on the Vygotskian theory, the basic assumptions of the sociocultural approach become appreciated. The zones of proximal development and dialogic education provide deaf education new ways of rendering appropriate education within constructionism.

—————➤∘◀—————

— Chapter 4 —

Constructionism: A Sociocultural Approach to Deaf Education*

Fran Hagstrom, Ph.D.
University of Arkansas

The goal of this chapter is to introduce the sociocultural approach to professionals in deaf education, and to recommend it as a basis for educational practices. An overview of the sociocultural approach and the implications of this for dialogic education will follow a brief summary of Vygotskian theory. The premises of the sociocultural approach will then be outlined for deaf education.

Constructivist education differs from the traditional approach in that it adheres to the belief that to learn, children must actively participate in the process of learning as they make sense out of what they are doing (Kikas & Hagstrom, 1993). | *Constructionist education* | Teachers are responsible for creating situations that facilitate learning because sense making depends on establishing learning environments and procedures that support active learning and the co-construction of knowledge between teachers and children (Dollard, 1996). The most attractive arena for making sense is an individual's daily world or ecology (Bronfenbrenner, 1979).

Participating in constructivist education requires teachers to use different skills than those that are characteristic of a more traditional approach. Within the traditional paradigm, teachers | *Traditional education* | select program materials designed for particular ages and/or grades, and use these serialized materials to direct learning. In contrast, teachers working in a constructivist paradigm

* The author wishes to thank John Muma for suggesting and encouraging the writing of this chapter, and Michael Holquist for comments on an early version of it.

select materials that can be used in a variety of ways and in no particular order, since these are used as tools for interaction that allow for individualized education within the classroom setting (Bodrova & Leong, 1996).

The educational roles for each of these two approaches are quite different. Traditionally, the teacher needs to know the developmental age and stage expectations for her grade level to select materials. In con-

| *Teacher's role changes* |

structionism, the teacher must have solid, theoretical understandings of how children learn and develop, since the use of any materials is individualized and vested in a child's intent during the dynamic of teaching and learning.

Just as the selection and use of materials differ between these two paradigms, so do the approaches in **adaptive education**. Simply giving

| *Adaptive education* |

less work or more time to complete work is often the approach in adaptive education in the traditional paradigm. This "lowering of the bar" to increase performance leads to little change or gain in understanding or learning if the child lacks "basic jumping skills" (Garmston & Wellman, 1999). Adaptive education in the constructivist paradigm is grounded in how children learn. It deals with things like basic jumping skills. Materials, procedures, and interactions are modulated to what and how a student understands something. Teaching and learning function as a dynamic that gives rise to a learning zone as teachers offer forms of assistance to support learning.

Traditional education is increasingly challenged by constructivist approaches. Rather than working within a maintained zone of sense making, the child's "ear," or lack thereof, is the focal point (Mayer & Wells,

| *The learner is not independent of the educational system.* |

1996; Tucker, 1999). The logic behind this might go something like this: Formal schooling depends on learning to read and write. Successful reading and writing depends on mastering the sound-symbol code of a spoken language. The ear conducts the sound that will be linked to the symbols of the code to the brain where such information is processed. Therefore, what the ear should do (e.g., provide the sound features needed for mastery of the code) becomes the focus of adaptive education when children who are hard of hearing are schooled. Approached from a traditional educational perspective, children would be given smaller chunks of work and longer periods of practice time to master the codes of language, reading, and writing. This logic has historical roots in the language development literature (localization theories of brain functioning and Chomskian-based theories of language development, Loritz, 1999). The fundamental perception from this perspective is that the physical individual as a separate and self-contained developing unit is what is tested, treated, and educated.

Sociocultural constructivist education is not built on such perceptions. Rather, while the concept of individuals as entities is assumed, social interaction that scaffolds the use of culturally designated tools is the focus of development (Hagstrom, 2000; Wertsch, 1991; Wertsch & Rupert, 1993). The movement from other-regulated to self-regulated learning and the forms of assistance needed to function within social interactions (including reading and writing in the classroom and community) are the focus of testing and treatment (Hagstrom). Adaptive education approached from this constructivist paradigm means that teachers should focus on intentional behavior whereby learning becomes invested in social interactions.

> *Sociocultural education is invested in social interaction.*

For example, teachers from the traditional approach are concerned with monitoring and controlling student behavior. However, constructionist-oriented teachers want to assist students to explore and think about how to organize the class so that learning is more efficient while meeting their respective needs. Toward that end, students want to contribute to the organization and functioning of the classroom. Constructionist teachers encourage their students to play active roles in the daily conduct of the class (DeVries, Zan, Hildebrandt, Edmiaston, & Sales, 2002; Vacca & Raisinski, 1992).

> *Students should assume active roles in their education.*

Basic Vygotsky

Understanding Vygotskian theory is pivotal to moving toward a sociocultural constructivist approach in deaf education. This view began to appear in the professional literature in the 1960s with the publication in America of Vygotsky's (1962) *Thought and Language*. In general, Vygotskian theory

> *Vygotskian theory has continuity with sociocultural education.*

is concerned with the social, cultural, and historical basis of individual mental functioning (Wertsch, 1985). While the theory has been used for comparative studies of gender, the workplace, and literacy among other things (Martin, Nelson, & Tobach, 1995), it has been incorporated most extensively in the field of education. Bruner (1990) used it to frame his discussion of how education is a culture that supports particular kinds of interactions. Others have used it to develop programs for children unaccustomed to formal schooling, those having difficulty succeeding in the classroom, and to provide a developmentally sound basis for instruction (Berk & Winsler, 1995; Forman, Minick, & Stone, 1993; Hicks, 1997; Moll, 1990).

There are three basic aspects to the Vygotskian theory. The first of these is his general position on **ontological development of mental functioning** (Vygotsky, 1987). Mental functioning of the child begins externally (intermentally) in the socially organized cultural world. What is first intermental (between people) becomes intramental (the child's own) as the child, with the assistance of social others, masters and appropriates tools for thinking and acting (Wertsch, 1985, 1991). This position on mental functioning stands in contrast to those that assume that the child develops certain cognitive skills before being aware of or using them with other people (Piaget, 1926). Here, skills begin in the social realm, in use with others, and then become the child's own. Such a developmental position places a good deal of emphasis on the role of other people and social interaction in the life of the young child (Nelson, 1996; Rogoff, 1990).

> *Learning begins intermentally (socially), then shifts to intramental learning (individual's possible worlds).*

Social interaction is well documented in deaf education when doing dialogue journal writing. In dialogue journal writing, the teacher and student correspond in an interactive journal, reflecting on experiences, feelings, and attitudes. Through the nonthreatening, conversational interaction of these journal entries, the teacher provides language models for engaging the child in intentional dialogue (Teller & Harriss, 1991).

> *Dialogue journal writing is one way to launch social based learning.*

The second aspect of Vygotskian theory that is important for constructivist education generates a position on how **language transforms**

thinking. Vygotsky (1987) claimed that two lines of development, which progress but are not initially intermingled, comprise the mental functioning of the young child. Biologically driven changes impact the young child's sensory systems while at the same time language is being acquired in conjunction with living in a socially passed down cultural world. These two lines of development, biological and language in social interaction, come together when the child reaches the point of consciously using language. Biologically organized ways of perceiving, sustaining attention, and figuring out how to maneuver in space and with things and others become transformed as these are mediated by language. With this shift, the child increasingly uses language to regulate things like attending and problem solving, and to restructure and structure remembering. This basic tenet is called Vygotsky's law of general cultural development (Vygotsky, 1987).

> *Biologically driven learning coupled with language acquisition results in conscious learning.*

The third Vygotskian developmental premise is his theory about **how children learn.** Vygotsky opposed standardized testing on the grounds that it does not address learning in developmentally sound ways. It was his position that what a child achieves on a standardized test reflects what has already been mastered and therefore exists as "fossilized" knowledge (Vygotsky, 1978; 1993). While this has important uses within many societies, it is insufficient information for assessing how a child learns, which was Vygotsky's developmental interest. Vygotsky (1978) claimed that children's learning progresses within "zones of proximal development" (ZPD).

> *Learning progresses within a zone of proximal development whereby the learner benefits from the assistance of others.*

If teachers work on material that the child has already mastered, although speed may increase, understanding and learning are not advanced. Similarly, if the skills worked on are so far above what a child can do even with assistance, there will be no change in understanding. Therefore, teaching and learning are developmentally sound when skills are attuned to what a child can just begin to master and understand, and if assistance is provided by teachers (or more knowledgeable/experienced peers) until the child can increasingly do these

> *Teachers should be attuned to what their students can do.*

things alone. Learning within the ZPD is not about moving to increasingly more difficult work but instead being able to complete work independently at a particular level of complexity that once required assistance (Hagstrom, 2000). As this kind of mastery builds, task complexity is increased so that teachers and learners are always generating and working within developmentally appropriate learning zones. Vygotsky's complaint about standardized tests was not that they did not serve a societal function but rather that they did not serve a developmental learning function. Developmentally appropriate assessment should, in addition to informing educators about what the child can do alone, describe what can be done with assistance and what cannot be done even with assistance.

In summary, Vygotskian theory, which is concerned with the mental development, provided a theoretical basis for the process of educating children regardless of physical or cultural differences. It did not address what should be learned, or when something should be learned. Rather, it described the fundamentals of a teaching-learning relationship that is applicable across situations, contexts, and cultures. As such, it is a basis for constructive education that focuses on how formal schooling can proceed.

The Sociocultural Approach

The sociocultural approach has its roots in Vygotsky's developmental theory. Those working from a sociocultural perspective assume that independent action exists first and foremost as interaction with others, and that it is socially, historically, and culturally situated. Contrary to Vygotsky's unit of analysis (i.e., language), Wertsch and his colleagues hold that the irreducible unit is always the individual plus what is used to complete an act. If the act is talking, it is the individual plus the language being used; if one has impaired hearing, the act is listening, and it is the individual plus the hearing aid, speechreading, and signed comprehension; and if it is word processing, it is the individual plus the software plus the hardware, and so forth. In this way mental functioning always extends beyond the skin of the individual (Wertsch, Tulviste, & Hagstrom, 1993). As can be seen, when using the "individual-acting-with-cultural tools" (IACT)(Wertsch & Rupert, 1993) as the unit of analysis, the physical individual as "what" is

> *Initial learning is socially, historically, and culturally situated.*

tested, treated, or schooled is not the focus since children cannot be described independent of the cultural tools they use for action. Furthermore, since action is always mediated, it is action in its mediated form (Wertsch, 1998; Wertsch, Tulviste, & Hagstrom) that can be observed and changed whether the educational task is assessment or learning in the classroom.

This sociocultural unit of analysis is particularly effective when working with those who require adaptive education, because what is gathered as empirical data must always extend beyond the physicality of the individual and include the means (mental, physical, or animate) used to accomplish tasks. The individual's handicapping condition is not the target of assessment and intervention but rather the individual's use of "tools" in context, be they physical ones such as glasses, hearing aids, cochlear implants, or wheelchairs; animate ones such as care-givers, teachers, or guide-dogs; and/or mental ones such as memory strategies, routines, or narratives (Hagstrom, 2000). This unit of analysis provides a structure for documenting developmental change, a fundamental task within the sociocultural approach.

> *Learning is regarded as the product of what the individual brings to the task and the means of learning.*

There is a second way that the sociocultural approach extends Vygotskian theory. It has taken on a particular direction as Wertsch (1991, 1998) and others have integrated issues of **dialogicality** (Bivens & Hagstrom, 1992; Cazden, 1993; Dore, 1989; Rommetveit, 1992). This is a Bakhtinian (1981) concept used to convey the notion that when individuals speak or write, they use the words and ideas of others for communication and perspective taking. Dore applied this perspective to language acquisition, and Nelson (1996) incorporated it into her theoretical position on cognitive development, while Cazden explored its implications for children participating in formal schooling.

> *Dialogicality means that when individuals think or use language they use concepts, ideas, and words of others.*

Within Wertsch's (1991, 1998) sociocultural approach, **dialogicality** is an essential notion because those things that mediate action inherently come with social and cultural "voice" that continues to be present even when they are used uniquely by

> *Thinking and language have a social and cultural "voice."*

individuals. As he states, "[V]irtually every text is viewed as involving both univocal, and hence intersubjectivity, as well as dialogic, thought-generating tendencies, and hence alterity" (Wertsch, 1998, p. 117). An individual's action with any cultural tool progresses from less to more skillful, and from being understood (by the individual) as univocal to multivoiced to dialogic. Wertsch addresses this progression by introducing the notions of mastery and appropriation into the sociocultural conceptualization of mind.

Mastery is generally thought of as a process that moves skill development from a basic introduction of material to command of the material evidenced in superior skills (Merriam-Webster, 1974).

> *Mastery pertains to the progress from initial entry to command of a given skill or learned domain.*

For example, the complex activity of concert performance begins with the simple act of learning where and how to place one's hands on the keys of a piano. Learning that there are things called letters that have names and sounds associated with them precedes the independent reading of stories, histories, or written mathematical problems. Efficient fingering, knowing which piano keys correspond to musical notes, which sounds go with which letters, and later on which style of writing corresponds to various knowledge domains are part of the declarative aspect of the mastery process. The sociocultural notion of mastery synthesizes the procedural aspect of learning with such declarative information so that mastery is understood as a process of "knowing how to use a mediational means (i.e., cultural tool) with facility" (Wertsch, 1998, p. 52). During this process the integration of new material into what is known, reflects back on what still needs to be mastered, and changes the individual's perspective of that which is being learned. Mastery depends on an individual actively continuing to participate in tasks as they become increasingly complex.

> *Appropriation is the process, in the course of learning, whereby the learner takes something that belongs to others and makes it his or her own.*

Appropriation occurs within the process of mastery. Wertsch (1998) uses this Bakhtinian term to designate the "process of taking something that belongs to others and making it one's own" (p. 53). Appropriation moves from unconscious use of cultural tools such as words, phrases, utterance, discourse, and opinions of others to increasingly conscious selection of these, and choices about where and how they are employed. For example, early in the mastery process children (or learners of any age) may use what is being taught to them as if it is the sole and only truth of their own invention. Lotmann (1988) referred to this as the univocal function of such texts. Yet to the listener, the looker, the teacher, the parent, and others, it is obvious that the child (learner) is saying (or doing) what has been said (or done) with them. Appropriation becomes more complex during mastery as the individual learner becomes conscious of the material only being partly his or hers, a multivoiced function (Lotmann). Learners progress to understanding that the routines, words, opinions, values, discourses, and so on are also someone else's, and that they are using these in concert with others or using them uniquely in perhaps a different context than the original. The change from thinking something is one's own, a univocal function, to understanding that only the employment is individual, a multivoiced function, signals shifts in appropriation within the mastery process.

The Baktinian end-point for mastery as it relates to the development of mind might be what Holquist (2001) calls **simultaneity**. This notion is grounded in the Bakhtinian position that nothing is ever "not dialogic." Words and actions are simultaneously those of the individual as well as that of various cultures and societal institutions. As such, they serve a dialogic, thought-generating function for the individual (Wertsch, 1998). This does not mean such social texts are not the individual's. It is just that they are also the others, all the others, who put them into societal use or who have kept them there. Specifically, since utterances overflow with the words, phrases, sentences, discourses, and texts of others (Hunt, 1994), all things individual are at the same time inexorably com-

> *With simultaneity, thoughts, concepts, and learning are mutually manifest in one's social bearing and culture.*

posed of and form a dialogue with what others have said or written. While simultaneity is, theoretically, always present and a part of individual action, children do not begin knowing or realizing this as they use language or learn in school. It is the individual's consciousness and use of the interrelatedeness of things to generate thought during the process of mastery that may be the most complex developmental aspect of mediated action. In other words, knowing that one's action is mediated and that all mediation comes with a historical tension during use may be the desired end-point for complex individual action in an increasingly complex global world. As such, simultaneity may function as a developmental telos that organizes activities, especially in contexts such as formal schooling.

In summary, the sociocultural approach extends Vygotskian theory with elaboration of the "individual-acting-with-cultural tools" as a unit of analysis, and the incorporation of dialogicality. These extensions of Vygotskian theory are particularly important in education since they can transform understanding what formal schooling is about, beyond the learning of basic codes, and expand what must be assessed and taught in addition to the mastery of these fundamentals. Within the context of formal schooling, children gain tools to perceive, understand, and be dialogic, but only if dialogicality is understood and included as an educational necessity.

Dialogicality in Education

> *The ultimate goal for dialogicality is an individual who functions appropriately in that person's society.*

Dialogicality as a developmental premise and an educational imperative intersect in issues of formal schooling. The goal of learning to read, write, and use language in school is not simply to master these skills to a measurable level on achievement tests, but to master them in order to think and reason in the service of functioning productively in society.

What constitutes "good" education is either an explicit or implicit part of any dialogue engaged in by parents, schools, teachers, and students. Measures used to describe change in student learning are reflections of the belief systems held by teachers, administrators, school districts, policy makers, and so on.

> *The force of authority in education is the belief system that underwrites education.*

Cheyne and Tarulli (1999) call these belief systems "the force of authority." When exemplified in local and/or national educational policy, this becomes part of a dialogicality hidden in the discourses of schools, and one that children and teachers must recognize to be educationally successful. In their opinion, constructivist teachers must be responsive to the emerging capacities of children since each child's educational characteristics depend on the character, abilities, and agenda of the teacher. The teacher's agenda, to be effective, must adhere to a curriculum that has the force of authority which guides schooling toward an idealized end-point (Cheyne & Tarulli). In other words, the development of the student, the skill of the teacher, and the force of authority triangulate to generate a dialogic **ZPD (zone of proximal development)** in successful education.

Sidorkin (1999) discusses good education as dialogic education. Citing Bakhtin's (1986) claim that it is through dialogue used communicatively that a person comes to be known and to exist, he suggested that schools should have the purpose of introducing children to the life of dialogue. This goal for education depends on dialogue being understood

> *Good education is dialogic education.*

as a central fact of human existence, a developmental position, and fundamental to good schooling, an educational position.

Using classroom data, Sidorkin (1999) described discourses that emerged when education was dialogic. These included an authoritative discourse produced by the teacher for what must be answered, a discourse of disruption where the student confronts the authoritative discourse explicitly or implicitly during the learning process, and a discourse of dialogic enactment where there is a lack of resolu-

> *Dialogic education can change the belief system of education.*

tion but acceptance of differences as students and teachers put authoritative and disruptive discourses in relationship. As can be seen, Sidorkin's work on dialogic education reflects the position that formal schooling must include learning about how to live in a human community as well as mastering reading, writing, and schoolized ways of using language. In a sense, he is attempting to influence the force of authority addressed by Cheyne and Tarulli (1999).

Two aspects of dialogicality with regard to education can be abstracted from these accounts. Sidorkin (1999) makes the case for the necessity of dialogicality as part of the force of authority. And Cheyne and Tarulli (1999), using Vygotsky's notion of ZPDs, outline the task of the constructive teacher in such an enterprise. Both of these are harmonious with the child's developing dialogicality within the sociocultural approach.

Organizing ZPDs for Deaf Education

The child who is learning to read, write, and use language in schoolized ways is also learning about what it means to learn and what is

> *Dialogic education is grounded in the value system of one's culture.*

important about learning according to parents, teachers, and society in the process. The former are part of the skills learned in school while the latter are parts of the dialogue that will frame the use of the skills, and both are essential aspects of a dialogic education. Having postulated the importance of dialogic education not only as an educational imperative within modern society, but also as an essential aspect of the child's mental development, those who educate children must have ways to think about and describe student progress. Documentation of three interactive ZPDs that organize ongoing, dialogic education can be used for this purpose.

The first of these ZPDs involve the learning of **the kinds of fundamental information** expected in formal schooling. This is characteristic

> *The nature of learning in any given task entails knowing what the learner can do and what assistance would be useful.*

of much of the research and writing that has been done on ZPDs that focuses on how children learn (Berk & Wisler, 1995; Bivens & Berk, 1990; Bodrova & Leong, 1996; Palincsar & Brown, 1984). Specifically, learners interact with teachers and peers through educational material to learn to read, write, do mathematics, build vocabulary, and so on. Teachers adjust levels of material complexity and forms of assistance so that

children can succeed in tasks, and children proceed to do things independently that they could at first do only with assistance (Hagstrom, 2000). For example, children learn to say the letters of the alphabet and their sound correlations by repeating after the teacher, working with pictures and letters in books, watching themselves in mirrors, and so forth. With basic proficiency, they can recite the alphabet when called upon in the classroom, but may need help getting started if the alphabet is requested as part of a new activity or in a new context. They need less assistance to move between activities and context with what they know as their skills improve. This is evident as children spontaneously identify letters they see, and work out the sounds of letters in new words not only at school but also at home, in stores, and in community settings. Children progress with mastery of the basic codes of reading, writing, and speaking until these seem as natural and as thoughtlessly engaged in as eating or breathing. To describe how and at what levels of difficulty children are working as they acquire the fundamentals introduced in the classroom, teachers can document the forms of assistance they give and those used by the child to complete tasks and participate in activities.

An additional ZPD concerns **mediated action**. The educational goal is for children to go beyond recognizing codes to knowing how to access, gain, and use information and, ultimately, understand its inherent dialogicality. This allows children to recognize that the particulars of any knowledge domain are dynamic in use as well as over time. The physical, mental, and animate tools provided by teachers so that children can master basic codes in classrooms are essential to the task of assisting children to understand the univocal function of the material they are mastering, move toward the multivoiced function, and reach the dialogic function. The student must move within skill

> *Education is not only learning content but also how to go beyond content so students can function independently.*

building from simple mastery (a declarative, univocal function), to fluent use of codes (integrating declarative knowledge with procedural knowledge), to perceiving that the codes are simultaneously theirs and others' (a multivoiced, analytical function), and then employ such knowledge with facility to effectively act in and on the world within varying contexts (analytically organizing declarative and procedural knowledge to function dialogically) (Rosner, 2001).

If this ZPD for mediated action is incorporated with the prior one for skill building, student progress might look something like this. The child treats the code being mastered as an exclusive possession that can be shown to others at will or upon request (univocal function). As learning continues, these same codes become a means for the child to gain information. This frames meaning, and becomes a lens through which the child perceives situations and social others (multivoiced function). Finally the code becomes a

> *Previous learning comprises a code by which further learning can be achieved.*

tool for creating meaning and new information that can be used to talk with oneself in the social voice carried by the previous uses of the code, and for interacting with social others in new ways (dialogic function).

The last of these ZPDs involve Cheyne and Tarulli's (1999) **force of authority**, characterized in the classroom by the kinds of discursive action described by Sidorkin (1999). Students may enter the classroom believing they know what they know, and give answers at school that

Learning is a socially negotiated enterprise.

would be the same as answers in the everyday world in which they have been functioning. The learner may then move to knowing what the teacher wants them to know, and give the kinds of answers expected by the teacher. The dialogic functioning begins as learners start to object to teacher-directed tasks or information provided by the teacher. This may take the form of not working; laughing, joking, or talking out in class; or directly disagreeing with the teacher (Sidorkin). As dialogic education proceeds within the classroom, learners and teachers negotiate expected answers and possible exceptions. Learners redefine and restate their answers in a variety of ways in tandem with responsive teaching where qualitative adjustments are made through rehashing, refining, and rephrasing. Learners move to knowing that what the teacher wants them to know is essential for succeeding in a social world that demands that these kinds of things be known, and at the same time knowing that they have the skills to reshape knowledge (Cheyne & Tarulli).

These three ZPDs are continuously being created, varied, and interwoven in the constructivist classroom. Dialogic education results as shifts occur among them. Teachers know what they want the child to learn as mandated by the external force of authority (Cheyne & Tarulli, 1999). They make sure of the developmental level of the child to do this. What

Teachers should scaffold the learning environment to assist learning.

the child can do alone and what the child can do as the teacher scaffolds the child's learning toward the culturally organized educational telos reflect these developmental levels (Hagstrom, 2000; Wertsch, 1998). The teacher scaffolds by means of selecting, organizing, and presenting suitable tasks that allow for the teaching of emerging skills. This requires ongoing evaluation of the task's suitability to its purpose; generating and maintaining student interest in the task; using modeling, questioning, and explanation to clarify the goals of the task; and presenting approximations and appropriate approaches as strategies to complete the tasks (Cheyne & Tarulli).

Documenting shifts from other- to joint- to self-regulation across these three ZPDs can serve as documentation of student progress. The range of educational complexity is anchored by mastery that has within it the concepts of appropriation and simultaneity, both of which hinge on movement from unconscious to conscious use of mediational means (Wertsch,

1998). For each new domain of knowledge, teachers can document students' ventriloquation of teacher and textbook explanations and note if this is used as what solely constitutes knowing the material covered in lessons. They can note when and document how students integrate personal understanding with the texts of the classroom and the talk of the teacher. And, since dialogicality becomes observable as it is constructed with others within the activities of the classroom, they can document where, when, and how

> *Documentation of learning can be achieved by citing specific instances whereby learning was other-oriented, jointly shared, and then self-regulated.*

students use reading, writing, and language to add their voices to others, and to challenge and compare ideas across the curriculum. Teaching and learning in ZPDs sensitive to the goal of dialogicality becomes a mechanism for students to continue to move through this cycle of learning throughout formal schooling. Increased awareness of one's mediational means has an identifiable history of use and meaning that, in turn, leads to changes in dialogic functions.

The Sociocultural Approach and Deaf Education

Dialogicality is a central feature of the sociocultural approach to mental functioning, and is the basis for one approach to constructivist education. The positions on the importance of dialogicality as a focus of education outlined above and the description of student change within such a position, are crucial for deaf education if learning is expected to move beyond the level of skill mastery to the discourses of literacies that are emerging in the modern world (Galin & Latchaw, 1998). Teachers of persons who are deaf or hard of hearing must recognize the importance of working within ZPDS, and of working toward dialogicality with their students even as basic skills are being taught and mastered. It is essential that they recognize that within any ZPD there is dialogicality. Teachers know what they want children to learn. The external force of authority that establishes funding and educational criteria often prescribes what should be learned. As they deal with the dialogicality of their

> *Education is a dynamic enterprise whereby both teacher and learner play active roles.*

own beliefs about educating children who are deaf or hard of hearing and this force of authority, teachers of the deaf and hard of hearing should engage in the practices of constructivist education, and work toward the goal of dialogic education. Teachers committed to teaching and learning as a dynamic must begin each session working from what makes sense to the child, moving the child to knowing what the teacher wants them to know, and leading them to engage in the discourses of formal education so that they can make sense of and come to know that what the teacher wants them to know is essential for succeeding in a social world.

———≫·0·≪———

The recent scholarly literature has documented the progressive and benefi-cial shift from behaviorism and reinforcement theory to constructionism and the centrality of intent as viable guides for language acquisition and teaching. Another closely related shift is occurring in the move away from the modality view of language to the CCCE view. These shifts provide deaf education with new perspectives on teaching and rendering appropriate services to individuals who are deaf and hard of hearing.

———≫·0·≪———

— Chapter 5 —

Constructionism: From Reinforcement to Intent

Henry Teller, Ed.D.
University of Southern Mississippi

For at least the past thirty-five years, special education, including deaf education, has held on tenaciously to reinforcement as a presumptive account of learning even at the cost of ignoring alternative views of learning issuing from constructionism (Bruner, 1981, 1986; Searle, 1992). This more recent scholarly literature has all but dismissed reinforcement as a viable account of learning in general, and language acquisition in particular (Bruner, 1981, 1986; Cazden, 1988; Muma, 1998; Nelson, 1985; Olson & Bruner, 1996; Paul, 2001; Searle, 1992). "Models of language acquisition built explicitly on assumptions of positive and negative reinforcement are no longer acceptable" (Nelson, 1985, p. 33). Yet, one has only to visit classrooms for deaf and hard of hearing students and/or residential schools for the deaf to observe that reinforcement (Do this, and you'll get that) continues to be a mainstay of language instruction as well as academic instruction.

> *Even though reinforcement has been dismissed, it is still widely used in deaf education.*

Kohn (1993), Muma (1998), Searle (1992), and others have documented the fundamental flaws with reinforcement as a viable account of language acquisition. Indeed, Bruner (1978) regarded positivism (reinforcement) as "corrosive dogma." These flaws include: failure to appreciate the centrality of intent or any mental state, silence about language acquisition sequences, available repertoires, active loci of learning, reliance on

> *Reinforcement accounts have been regarded as "corrosive dogma."*

frequencies (or percentages) as presumed evidence of learning, and capricious decisions concerning content, sequence, and pacing in language acquisition. Paul (2001) contends that a major criticism of behaviorism is the fact that there is almost no consideration for what the child brings to the language-learning task (intent and repertoire).

Language Acquisition:
The Behavioristic Perspective

Watson, the father of empiricism, is generally considered the father of behaviorism. His attempt to account for the behavior of both man and animals in purely physiological and physical terms was discussed in his 1919 text, *Psychology from the Standpoint of a Behaviorist.* Watson argued that behavior is objective and observable and that the agenda for psychology consists of formulating laws relating stimulus conditions to behavior. Consciousness, introspection, and the mind were to play no role in this science of behavior (Medlin & Ross, 1992; Searle, 1992).

> *Behaviorists believe that behavior is objective and observable.*

Over the last fifty years, there has been a decline in the influence of behaviorism due in part to the publication of Chomsky's (1959) *Review of Skinner's Verbal Behavior in Language.* Chomsky (1959, 1968) comments that behaviorism provides an inadequate account of language acquisition. Yet, as stated above, behaviorism still exerts a great influence in special education, including language instruction with children who are deaf and hard of hearing. Behaviorism is especially prevalent in language studies that emphasize the importance of spoken or signed expressions and the role of the social environment (Paul, 2001).

Although behaviorism is richly evident in claimed accounts of language acquisition and instruction, it is not considered to be a viable account of these processes today according to the major language scholars. Bruner (1978, 1986) indicated that reinforcement theory has seen its day. Muma and Teller (2001) and Searle (1992) cite fundamental flaws in reinforcement, including a failure to appreciate the centrality of intent or any mental state of the learner. Cazden (1972) states that reinforcement

> *A review of the literature on parent-child interaction showed that reinforcement did not exist.*

has merely provided an educational procedure for making teachers operational, even though the more substantial issue is to what extent such procedures are appropriate. Furthermore, Cazden (1988) comments, "To put the conclusions bluntly: Reinforcement did not exist, frequency did not correlate, and expansions did not help" (p. 28).

Behaviorists consider the child to be a passive learner waiting to receive and accumulate information. In contrast, constructionism holds that children are active learners. With behaviorist teaching, the child will eventually think of learning experiences as "What do you want me to do, and what do I get for doing it?" Or "What do you want me to do, and what happens to me if I don't do it?" Rewards comprise the operating premise of behaviorism, irrespective of intent or intrinsic motivation (Kohn, 1993; Muma & Teller, 2001).

> *Behaviorists regard a child as a passive learner waiting to be taught.*

One may ask, "If behaviorism, especially its reinforcement/rewards component, does not work, why are special educators still using it?" Behaviorism, in fact, does work—but only for the short term. It gets temporary compliance, but it does not help students to value what they are doing. In fact, the research shows that the more people are rewarded for doing something, the more they come to lose interest in whatever they had to do to get the reward (Kohn, 1993).

> *Reinforcement may have short-term effects.*

Lepper, Greene, and Nisbett (1973) conducted a study with preschool children in California. Fifty-one preschoolers were observed as they drew creatively with colored markers. Some were told they would receive rewards in the form of a certificate with a ribbon and a gold star for drawing—something children of this age seem to enjoy naturally—and the others were not rewarded. After several days those children who had been told in advance of the certificate they would receive seemed to be less interested in drawing with markers than the other children who were not rewarded—and less interested than they themselves had been before the reward was offered. Kohn (1993) commented on the failure of summer reading promotions by libraries and a national campaign by Pizza Hut to entice children to read by offering them baseball cards, pizza, movie

> *Programs that require students to perform in particular ways typically have short-term effects.*

passes, and other prizes for reading books. Does reading to obtain a reward produce children who learn to love books? The rewards do buy the behavior—checking out and reading a book—but at what cost? Reading was not represented as an enjoyable experience but as a task one must complete to obtain a goody.

An investigation by Schwartz (1982) of a similar promotion found that the books children chose to read in the promotions tended to be short and simple ones with large type. The books were selected because it appeared that they could be read quickly. Personal interest in a book's content was not a consideration.

When a child is engaged in literacy or academic activities with the focus on receiving a reward for efforts to read, risk taking is greatly inhibited. Kohn (1993) indicated that ". . . when we are working for a reward, we do exactly what is necessary to get it and no more" (p. 63). Children are less likely to take chances, play with possibilities, or follow hunches. Kohn stated further, "Risks are to be avoided because the objective is not to engage in an open-ended encounter with ideas, it is to get the goody" (p. 63). Rewards also inhibit exploration. When getting the reward is the child's focus, the child is not likely to be flexible or innovative in problem solving. Children are most likely to stick with what produced the reinforcer (reward) before, because the reward is what the child is working to receive.

> *When the goal of learning is a sticker or ribbon, children typically take the shortest course rather than actually learn.*

Constructivism

As a philosophy of learning, constructivism can be traced at least to the eighteenth century and the work of the Neapolitan philosopher Giambattista Vico, who held that humans can only clearly understand what they have themselves constructed. In the twentieth century John Dewey, Lev Vygotsky, Jean Piaget, Jerome Bruner, Daniel Dennett, and others elaborated further on these views (Classroom Compass, 1995).

> *Learners understand what they have constructed.*

Dewey believed education depended on action. He held that knowledge and ideas emerged only from a situation in which learners had to draw from experiences that had meaning and importance to them. These situations had to occur in a social context, such as a classroom, where students joined in manipulating materials and, thus, created a community of learners who built their knowledge together (Classroom Compass, 1995).

> *It is desirable to have a community of learners working together.*

Piaget's (1973) constructivism is based on his view of the psychological development of children. He believed that the fundamental basis of learning was discovery. To Piaget, understanding came through discovery or reconstruction by rediscovering something. He viewed discovery

> *Discovery is an active learning enterprise.*

as the basis for production and creativity, and he equated other learning as the product of mere repetition.

Another important contributor to the constructionistic view was Vygotsky. Vygotsky (1962) believed that children learn scientific concepts out of a "tension" between their everyday notions and adult concepts. Faced with directives for learning, a child will only memorize what the adult said about the idea. To make it the learner's property, the child must use the concept and link that use to the idea as first represented meaningfully.

> *Children are faced with the decision of deciding whether to learn for the teacher or learn for themselves.*

Bruner (1986) is the foremost contemporary advocate of constructionism. Muma (1998), taking into account the works of Bruner, Nelson, Searle, and Vygotsky, explained constructivism:

> . . . the view that an individual actively constructs possible worlds [experientially defined knowledge of the world] and situated minds [biologically, cognitively, linguistically, socially, culturally, emotionally defined view of the world] by virtue of living in the world. Early constructions are evidently derived from embodiment . . . whereby schemas may be established. Such schemas are rudimentary notions [preconceptual in nature, Lakoff, 1987; Muma, 1998] of one's situated place in scripts and formats and they constitute early versions of event representations . . . or procedural knowledge.
> . . .The essence of constructionism is that an individual

> *Individuals actively construct their possible worlds and situated minds.*

from infancy throughout adulthood is an active learner in constructing possible worlds or a situated mind.

Language acquisition is thus grounded on what an individual knows of the world and actively constructs from intents. The scholarly literature has shown that what individuals think and communicate about is what they know and want or intend to do (Muma & Teller, 2001). Therefore, it is necessary to ascertain an individual's basic knowledge of the world, possible worlds (Bruner, 1986), experiential realism (Lakoff, 1987), or situated mind (Nelson, 1996). Importantly, these views are biologically, cognitively, linguistically, emotionally, socially, and culturally situated. The situated mind incorporated the social bases of language acquisition. From this Vygotskian perspective, it can be said that learning, in general, begins on a social level and then shifts to a personal level. This perspective is crucial, because it means that how the individual is socially and culturally situated are the defining issues for subsequent learning (Muma & Teller, 2001).

> *What individuals learn is directly governed by what they already know.*

It is thus vital that parents and educators of the deaf expand and vary the deaf child's experiential world toward establishing increased knowledge of the world and varying the child's social and emotional worlds as well. If this intervention does not occur, deaf children will tend to be socially and emotionally inactive, awkward, or isolated resulting in dependency on others rather than thinking and acting for themselves (Muma & Teller, 2001). Thus, there are three basic issues that should be the focus of deaf education: (a) expand the experiential base, (b) expand the social base, and (c) expand the emotional base.

> *It is desirable to expand and vary a learner's experiential, social, and emotional worlds.*

The two main communicative functions of language are intent and content. Intent, in fact, has emerged as the central issue in language acquisition (Bruner, 1986; Muma, 1998; Searle, 1992). In so doing, it has superseded reinforcement in providing a more viable account of language acquisition (Muma & Teller, 2001). Muma and Teller summarized this circumstance as follows:

> *Intent is the irreducible nucleus of language acquisition, and it has replaced reinforcement as a more viable account.*

Thus, it behooves deaf education to shift away from behaviorism and reinforcement toward the contemporary scholarly literature that supports the centrality of intent. The need for this shift is based not only on the necessity to become aligned with the scholarly literature but on the reality that so much of language assessment and intervention in deaf education is based on elicitation rather than intention. (p. 33)

There are two main kinds of content: explicit and implicit. Explicit content is the propositional nature of a message; that is, explicit content pertains to the basic ideas entailed in a message. In contrast, implicit content is an individual's knowledge of worlds, possible worlds, or the situated mind that makes explicit content meaningful.

> *Language acquisition pertains to the roles of implicit and explicit content of messages.*

The significance of these two kinds of content can be seen in the following sentence: "We will tack to port on the next header." Unless the reader is a sailor, this sentence is meaningless; that is, the reader does not have the necessary implicit knowledge to make this sentence meaningful. With this knowledge, however, the reader would know that *tack* is to change directions in a sailboat by turning the bow toward the wind and shifting the sails, that *port* is the left side of the boat when facing toward the bow, and that a *header* is a gust of wind. Thus, it is necessary to have both explicit and implicit knowledge in order to have a sentence work as intended (Muma & Teller, 2001). A counterexample may also be given relative to the individual familiar only with a sign language vernacular unique to a specific region of the country or a particular cultural within the greater Deaf community.

This distinction between explicit and implicit knowledge has implications for deaf education. It underscores again the need for enlarged and varied experiential and social bases of language. It also brings into question drill activities, such as rote vocabulary teaching, that deal with elicitation (Mandler, 1983; Muma & Teller, 2001).

> *The distinctions between implicit and explicit content bring into question the value of drill.*

Comprehension entails the planning and execution of messages (Clark & Clark, 1977). For example, an individual needs to decide what

Messages are constructed by making decisions about what should be implicit and explicit.

information should be implicit and what information should be explicit in order to make a particular intent recognizable. Comprehension requires the construction of possible propositions and utilizing these propositions within the context of what that individual knows of the world (Clark & Clark).

The literature on parallel processing has added greatly to this perspective (e.g., Anderson, 1983; Welman & Gelman,

Parallel processing pertains to the distinctions about implicit and explicit content.

1992). An example of parallel processing may be seen in the following sentence: The boy who won the race is my son. To process the idea that *the boy is my son* requires that one holds that thought in abeyance while the information that *the boy won the race* is processed and then integrated into the proposition.

Inasmuch as these mental processes may not be observed directly but inferred (Sperber & Wilson, 1986), it is necessary to provide evidence that warrants such inferences. Recognizing that spon-

Representative language samples provide evidence of an individual's repertoire, progress in sequences, strategies of learning, and active loci.

taneous signing or speech communication provides prima facie evidence of what an individual can do, it behooves professionals to obtain representative language samples that can be used to ascertain repertoires of grammatical and pragmatic skills, progress in acquisition sequences, strategies of learning, and active loci of learning. Such evidence is available in spontaneous language samples. Language tests do not have these capabilities (Muma, 1998; Muma & Teller, 2001).

Constructivism Applications

The main tenet of constructivism is that learning means construct-

Constructionism is constructing one's own knowledge as intended.

ing, creating, inventing, and developing one's own knowledge as intended. Others can give information, or information can be obtained from various sources such as libraries or on-line, but receiving information is not the same as learning. Learning, according to constructionists, includes the results of questioning, interpreting, and analyzing information. It also includes using the information to build and alter our meaning of previously held concepts and ideas and integrating one's own experiences about a given subject (Marlowe & Page, 1998).

Constructionists indicate that meaning and learning about issues, problems, and topics are based in large part on what an individual already knows. This prior knowledge affects how new events become interpreted and experienced. These interpretations provide a means of creating new knowledge (Marlowe & Page, 1998).

> *Previous knowledge governs what an individual can learn.*

Social and cultural influences also play a role. Such influences constitute major leveling effects whereby individuals ultimately share essentially similar views of the world.

Because meanings and understandings of issues, concepts, and problems are constructed by students, the constructivist classroom promotes learning

> *Social and cultural influences provide leveling effects between individuals.*

through students' intellectual activities such as questioning, investigating, problem generating, and problem solving. Constructing knowledge is the essence of knowing (Marlowe & Page, 1998).

A teacher with a constructivist view is concerned about thinking and the thinking process, rather than

> *Constructing knowledge is the essence of knowing.*

about the quantity of information a student can memorize and recite. Content is not devalued. Content is important; however, in a constructivist classroom, the teacher does not deliver most of the content material. It is the students who discover and reflect on content and their conceptions of such through inquiry, investigation, research, and analysis in the context of a problem, critical question, issue, or theme, and often within a social context such as small group activities. Students learn to think for themselves, and to think critically. They learn to discriminate between relevant and irrelevant data and to look at issues from various perspectives (Marlowe & Page, 1998).

> *When students discover and reflect on content, appropriate learning takes place.*

As important as information is, the passive accumulation of disconnected information is not learning. Passively receiving knowledge from
someone else is not learning. Learning requires that

> *Learning should
> not be reduced to
> teacher talk and
> student listening.*

the student be mentally, and often, physically active.
Students learn when they discover answers or relationships for themselves and create their own interpretations. Such learning is deeper, more comprehen-
sive, and long lasting. It leads to thinking critically (Marlowe & Page,
1998). According to Goodlad (1984), "Learning is not a lot of teacher talk
and a lot of student listening . . ." (p. 242).

Bruner's (1961, 1981, 1986) discovery theory strongly supports the
constructivism view. He believes that whatever a person discovers for
himself is what he truly knows. From discovery,

> *The act of
> discovery is the
> learner's doing.*

Bruner asserts, comes increased intellectual ability,
including the ability to solve problems. This discovery
is a matter of students thinking about and rearranging
material in terms of their interests and previous knowledge of the world.
For Bruner (1961), *schemata* refers to an open dynamic concept that holds
the potential for discovering new insights and new inquiries. The goal is
for students to be autonomous and self-propelled thinkers.

Boyer (1988), in his highly regarded *Carnegie Foundation Report*, concluded that if students are to excel, they must be engaged actively in
learning. They must become creative, independent thinkers, not passive
receivers of information.

In the elementary education classroom, the "Whole Language"
approach is compatible with the philosophy of constructivism (Marlowe
& Page, 1998), because this approach emphasizes that a child's experiences, interests, and needs should be central to the reading curriculum.

> *Whole Language
> is a
> constructionist
> approach.*

In Whole Language, new learning takes place when
students integrate new information with what they
already know. Whole Language classrooms also allow
children to make greater choices in what they read
and write about, and, in general, the children take the
lead as they pursue their own natural curiosities. Reading is viewed as a
developmental process that unfolds gradually and naturally as it is nur-
tured by teachers; practiced in shared, social environments; and modeled
by appropriate models. Meaning and comprehension are emphasized.

Skill development comes later as a natural progression (Marlowe & Page, 1998). While the Whole Language approach is constructionistic in philosophy, it has a major flaw in that it is conceptually weak by virtue of its ten principles which were merely authoritarian edicts (Goodman, 1986).

Kohn's Perspective

Kohn (1993) comments that one of the most disquieting things about American education is the emphasis placed on being quiet. In traditional classrooms, talking (and/or signing) is called "misbehaving." Such behavior is often deemed as an indication of lack of self-control or self-discipline, except when a pupil is recognized by the teacher for the purpose of giving a short answer to a factual question. Traditional programs expect students to sit quietly and listen. In the traditional Jug-and-Mug teaching philosophy, a teacher is viewed as the repository of knowledge and selectively

> *Traditional education may be regarded as the Jug-and-Mug approach.*

pours a little bit of information at a time into the empty vessel (a student). It is the student's job to retain passively the information—and now and then, to regurgitate some of it on command to provide evidence that some of it got in. The process is carried out by the deployment of rewards for success, punishments for failure, and an elaborate scoring system to keep track of presumed learning. Glasser (1990) comments that this model defines education by how many fragments of information students can retain long enough to be measured on standardized achievement tests.

Kohn (1993) offers an alternative and constructivist approach to the traditional behavioral-based teaching and learning that predominate in many schools. He terms it the **Three Cs—Collaboration** (Learning Together), **Content** (Things Worth Knowing), and **Choice** (Autonomy in the Classroom).

Collaboration. In collaborative (or cooperative) learning students work together in pairs, or small groups, instead of competing with each other for grades or prizes or trying to be the first to come up with the right answer. In a cooperative environment, students also develop more positive feelings about themselves, others, and the subject that they are studying. Wong and Wong (1998) indicated that

> *Collaboration occurs when students learn together.*

during cooperative learning activities, students clarify opinions, compare impressions, share solutions, and develop skills for leadership and teamwork. It is a win-win situation. It is successful because the context of the work group is more important than the content of the group. A caring and committed group of people working together will achieve the goal of the activity much more quickly than if each were to attempt the task alone (Wong & Wong).

Mueller and Fleming (2001) reviewed studies of cooperative learning within the schools over the past sixty-three years. They concluded that the benefits of cooperative or collaborative learning were "remarkable." The benefits of collaborative learning included improvement in intellectual and social skills and solutions to an array of educational problems. Mueller and Fleming also cited reports from the children themselves. These students stated emphatically that they learned better when they were "free to do something" in contrast to just reading the textbook and answering questions at the end of the chapter. Or as Caplow and Kardash (1995) view it, "knowledge is not transferred from expert to learner, but created and located in the learning environment" (p. 209).

> *The results of studies on collaboration are remarkable.*

Wong and Wong (1998) add that it is the responsibility of the teacher to facilitate the success of collaborative group work. It is as much cooperating to learn as it is learning to cooperate. Students have a vested interest in making sure that their group mates do well. Anything they do to help the group learn new skills benefits them all.

Cooperative learning promotes positive peer relationships, social skills, and self-esteem. When students work together cooperatively, they tend to like class better, they are more interested in the subject, and they have fewer discipline problems (Wong & Wong, 1998). Gould (1996) also stressed that real learning takes place when classrooms and curriculum are organized so that students can collaborate, interact, and raise questions of both classmates and teachers.

> *Collaborative learning promotes positive peer relationships, social skills, and self-esteem.*

Content. Kohn (1993) asserted that much of what students are required to do in school is of questionable value. Assigned tasks often involve very little creative thought and very much rote learning.

Children have difficulty connecting school content to their lives and interests, and educators may be losing them as learners, because they may be turned off by the whole process.

> *School content may be of questionable value in everyday life.*

Again, a constructivist approach appears to offer a better perspective. Instead of using behavioral techniques to try to keep students on task, one might ask, "What is the task? Is it worth doing?" Teachers should try to understand how children actively construct knowledge and weigh new information against their previous understandings.

It takes time and work to develop interesting lessons. Teachers may have to develop a sense of flexibility, a tolerance for unpredictability, and a willingness to give up absolute control of the classroom. It is easier to control when teaching is simply a matter of transferring disconnected facts and skills.

> *Teachers should be flexible, tolerant, and willing to share control with their students.*

An example may be gleaned from teaching reading. Shouldn't reading begin with the **content** about things students are interested in rather than the traditional basals and worksheets?

<u>Choice.</u> Kohn (1993) argues that if you deprive children of self-determination, they may lose their motivation to learn. If learning is a matter of following orders, students simply will not take to it in the way they would if they had some say about what they were doing. Giving

> *When students make choices, they learn better.*

students some **choices** about their learning works better than dictating everything children should do and when they should do it.

The benefits of allowing children to have input or **choice** into what they do in school are great. Amabile and Gitomer (1984) noted that when preschoolers were allowed to select the materials they used for making a collage, their work was judged more creative than the work of children who used exactly the same materials but did not get to choose them. deCharms (1972) found that when teachers of inner-city children were trained in a program designed to promote a sense of self-determination, the children in these classes missed less school and scored better on a national test of basic skills than those in conventional classrooms.

> *When children have opportunities to make choices, they not only learn better but enjoy learning.*

Boggiano, Shields, Barrett, Kellam, Thompson, Simons, and Katz (1992) found that children given more opportunity to participate in decisions about schoolwork scored higher on standardized tests. Condry (1977) found that when students were given autonomy in their assignments, they would continue working even on relatively uninteresting tasks. And Danner and Lonky (1981) found that when students were given autonomy in work choice, they tended to select assignments of an appropriate difficulty level so they would be properly challenged. Choice works.

Muma's CCCE Model

Muma and Teller (2001) described traditional deaf education as having a modality view of language whereby the expressive modalities (speaking, signing, writing) are thought to be crucially different from the receptive modalities (listening, lipreading, reading signs, reading). An accompanying perspective is that auditory or visual processing are deemed to be crucial.

> *The modality view is often part of traditional education.*

Muma and Teller (2001) further stated that the essential problem with the modality view of language is that it misses the core of language that is cognition, codification, communication, and expression (CCCE). Expression in this perspective refers to affect rather than modality. While there are modality differences, the core issues are essentially shared by all modalities and should have priority in rendering appropriate education. Regardless of modality, a sentence has essentially the same cognitive, communicative, and expressive functions.

> *The modality view misses the core CCCE aspects of language.*

Virtually all of the modern language scholars (Bloom, Bruner, Brown, Cazden, Chomsky, Clark & Clark, Gopnik, Grice, Macken, Nelson, Perera, Snow, Searle, Sperber, Wilson, and many others) solidly support the CCCE model. In contrast, it would be difficult to find these and other major scholars who place an emphasis on modality differences at the cost of missing the core CCCE issues. Indeed, Tallal (1990) summarized the research on auditory processing and concluded that mental processing of language is not modality-specific. Thus, rather than modality problems, individuals who evidence specific language impairment evidence difficulties that are not modality-specific. Tallal commented, "These deficits are neither specific to speech stimuli nor confined to the auditory modality. . . . The deficit in rapid temporal analysis and production is not specific to linguistic information per se, or to the auditory modality" (pp. 616-617). With a CCCE perspective, many of the views and practices would change toward more appropriate and effective teaching.

Constructivist principles applied specifically to the acquisition language in deaf children and other children with language difficulties are seen in the cognitive socialization approach that is oriented on CCCE (Muma, 1998). This approach views the intent of the speaker (signer) as the central issue in communication. Intent is also viewed as the basic issue in the contemporary constructionist movement

> *The CCCE perspective is a constructionist perspective.*

(Bruner, 1986; Searle, 1992) and speech acts and relevance theories. The individual from infancy throughout adulthood is seen as an active learner constructing possible worlds or a situated mind.

The primary tenet of cognitive socialization is that cognitive, social, emotional, and cultural influences have priority over structure, or, rather, structure is in the service of function. This tenet has major implications for language acquisition with children who are deaf or hard of hearing and offers a more appropriate alternative than the modality perspective. Likewise, the centrality of intent provides a more viable account of the development of language with all children, including those children who are deaf or hard of hearing.

> *Cognitive socialization deals with cognitive, social, emotional, and cultural influences.*

———⟫•◦•⟪———

The United States is becoming an increasingly multicultural society, and the Deaf culture is a part of that diversity, although the Deaf community often is overlooked by the hearing culture. This is because the Deaf community is a somewhat closed society, and hearing individuals are granted access to the culture infrequently (Higgins, 1980). The task of improving communication between the Deaf and hearing cultures may be accomplished from a cognitive socialization perspective. In understanding the cognitive socialization approach to language, deaf individuals and hearing persons may learn to communicate more effectively.

———⟫•◦•⟪———

— Chapter 6 —

Multicultural Language Issues: A Deaf Culture

Steven J. Cloud, Ph.D.
University of Southern Mississippi

The United States is becoming an increasingly multicultural society, and the Deaf culture is part of this diversity, although the Deaf community actually is shrinking, unlike most minority groups (Nuru-Holm & Battle, 1998). Yates (1988) wrote that "the political power and influence of minorities is undeniable in a nation which, by the year 2000, will have 260 million people, one of every three of whom will be either Black, Hispanic, or Asian-American" (p. 1). The most recent evidence compiled from the year *2000 U.S. Bureau of the Census* (U.S. Census Bureau, March 12, 2001) indicated that while Yates's figures were not completely accurate, diversity is increasing in this country. The latest data indicated that there is a total population of 281,421,906 in the United States, with individuals listing their race as White comprising 75.1% of that total. Other races responding included Hispanics or Latinos (12.5%—actually considered as an ethnic group and not a racial group), Blacks or African-Americans (12.3%), Asians (3.6%), American Indians or Alaskan Natives (0.9%), and Native Hawaiians and other Pacific Islanders (0.1%). Those reporting some other races (5.5%), and two or more races (2.4%), also responded to the census.

> *The United States is becoming increasingly multicultural.*

What these numbers do not reveal accurately, however, are the numerous subcultures in the United States that were not identified by the Bureau of the Census. These groups often use an in-group dialect, or language, which differs from Standard American English (SAE). Included in these subcultures are the

> *Subcultures often use dialects that differ from Standard American English.*

incarcerated, speakers of Appalachian English, prostitutes, the homeless, Cajun English speakers, gays and lesbians, gang members, and so on.

Perhaps one of the most frequently overlooked subgroups is the Deaf community. Many people are unaware that American Sign Language (ASL) is the fourth most commonly used language in the United States today, with more than 13 million deaf and hearing individuals using it to communicate (Costello, 2000). Unless one resides in a large metropolitan area, however, or unless there is a school for the deaf in one's neighborhood, it is unlikely that individuals using ASL in public will be seen. This is because the Deaf community is a somewhat closed society, and hearing individuals are granted access to this culture infrequently (Higgins, 1980).

> *ASL is the fourth most used language in the U.S.*

The National Center for Health Statistics (NCHS) of the U.S. Department of Health and Human Services periodically estimates the number of deaf or hard of hearing people residing in the United States. "According to their 1990 and 1991 Health Interview Surveys, approximately 20 million persons, or 8.6% of the total U.S. population 3 years and older, were reported to have hearing problems" (Holt, Hotto, & Cole, 1994, p. 2). This was the most recent information available from the Center for Assessment and Demographic Studies at Gallaudet University. It is likely that more recent demographic information will be made available as the year 2000 U.S. census data are analyzed.

> *About 20 million individuals in the U.S. have hearing difficulties.*

As stated previously, however, the deaf population in the United States actually is decreasing in size. Nuru-Holm and Battle (1998) reported that "In 1970, maternal rubella, mumps, and measles ranked as the major causes of hearing impairment. By 1980, mumps and measles had nearly disappeared, but rubella still occurred" (p. 359). Schildroth and Hotto (1993) determined that most cases of deafness today are due to hereditary factors, or to meningitis, because rubella is not as prevalent as it once was. Some individuals, however, suspect that deafness actually may increase in the future due to the influx of immigrants (legal and illegal) to the U.S., and due to the increased use of certain antibiotics to treat infants (Cloud, Buisson, & Hall, 2001).

> *The deaf population is decreasing in size.*

It is somewhat difficult for hearing individuals to gain acceptance in the Deaf community because the deaf usually are protective of their culture. When a hearing person becomes proficient in ASL, most deaf individuals are willing to engage them in manual communication. However, when they are not profi-cient, deaf individuals become frustrated in trying to sign exact English as a way to keep them abreast of the gist of the communication (Coulston, 1988). According to Lane (1992), deaf individuals also have a shared heritage of oppression, and they are somewhat

> *Individuals in the Deaf culture may distrust some individuals in the hearing culture.*

distrustful of the hearing population. Many deaf people maintain a neg-ative attitude toward hearing persons because they feel that members of the hearing community may try to take advantage of their deafness.

The Deaf community typically is comprised of a small group of indi-viduals in a given communicative setting. Surrounding this core group, which uses ASL as its primary mode of communication, there is a larger, hard of hearing community, which is provided varying degrees of access to the deaf core. Encompassing the hard of hearing group is the hearing community, which seldom interacts with the core group of deaf individ-uals unless there is a family member who also is a member of the Deaf community (see Figure 6.1).

Figure 6.1. The core Deaf community is surrounded by the hard of hearing community which, in turn, is encompassed by the hearing community.

There are three major problems inherent in intercultural contact (Cloud, 1998). They are ethnocentrism, ignorance, and intolerance. **Ethnocentrism** is "the emotional attitude that one's own race, nation, or culture is superior to all others" (Webster's New World Dictionary, 1968, p. 499). Ethnocentrism is common in this country. In American schools, children learn to speak, read, and write English. One recites the Pledge of Allegiance to the United States of America and sings American songs. Students take American history classes study American literature. Is it any wonder that many Americans maintain an ethnocentric view of the world? From the Deaf community's perspective, there is only one society in the United States—the hearing society—and the primary goal of this ethnocentric society is to mainstream deaf individuals into the hearing world's culture (Paul & Quigley, 1990).

> *Ethnocentrism is the emotional view that one's own race, nation, or culture is superior to all others.*

Ignorance also affects intercultural relations. Such ignorance does not occur due to a simple lack of education in most instances. Rather, it occurs because one culture lacks adequate knowledge of the other. Intelligent and educated people may make communication mistakes because they are ignorant of cultural norms and values. For example, when talking to a deaf person, one should speak as clearly as possible at a moderate pace and at moderate loudness levels. One never shouts because the increased intensity tends to distort speech, and it conveys a negative visual signal to the deaf listener (Zak, 1995). Most hearing individuals, however, subconsciously increase vocal intensity when speaking to a deaf person, just as they increase loudness levels when speaking to a foreigner.

> *Ignorance can play a disruptive role when hearing individuals deal with deaf or hard of hearing individuals.*

Finally, **intolerance** is a problem inherent in intercultural contact. In many instances, deaf and hearing individuals find it difficult to interact appropriately with one another primarily due to a communication gap and due to stereotyped impressions of the other's culture.

Researchers (Cole, 1989) have determined that it takes an approximate 15% minority insurgence into

> *Some hearing individuals may be intolerant of deaf and hard of hearing individuals who may not communicate well.*

a given community for the group to be assimilated and readily accepted. Apparently, when the minority population reaches this critical threshold, it becomes necessary for members of the majority culture to interact with them frequently in various social settings, in religious services, in the workplace, and in the community. Once the two cultures mingle and

> *About 15% minority insurgence is needed to achieve assimilation into a majority group.*

interact, then the stereotypes generally are recognized as such, and they begin to dissipate.

For effective communicative interactions to occur between deaf and hearing individuals, each should meet the other at least halfway. The deaf person might concede that it may be necessary to use an English-based sign system, such as Pidgin sign language (Vernon & Andrews, 1990) rather than ASL. The hearing individual should learn at least some rudimentary forms of ASL, or another manual form of expression. If effective communication is to occur, each individual should develop a knowledge base and an understanding of the language and cul-

> *It is necessary for both the hearing and the deaf or hard of hearing to accommodate each other.*

ture of the other (see Figure 6.2). This is a time-consuming and difficult process, particularly for the hearing person, who is unlikely to interact often with the Deaf community.

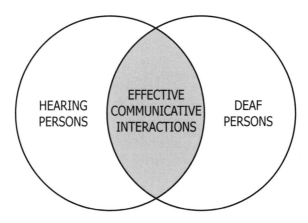

Figure 6.2. Deaf and hearing persons should meet each other halfway for effective communicative interactions.

The task of improving communication between the hearing and Deaf communities can be approached effectively from a cognitive socialization perspective. This widely accepted explanation of language development is endorsed by a number of experts to explain language development (Brown, 1956, 1973, 1986; Bruner, 1986; Muma, 1998; Nelson, 1996). Cognitive socialization addresses the importance of cognition, codification, communication, and emotion (affect) in the development of language skills. This view also is known as the CCCE perspective (Muma, 1998).

Cognition: Individuals from the hearing community assume that everyone thinks in words (Vernon & Andrews, 1990). According to Furth (1966) and Vander Woude (1970), however, verbal symbols may not mediate the thought processes. As a result, the cognitive aspects of communication should not differ between deaf and hearing individuals. Nelson (1996) disagreed with this view. She summarized the literature that showed that a child uses language to mediate knowledge of the world. Bloom (1973) suggested that cognition provides a base for language learning, and that when linguistic skills have advanced sufficiently, a crossover function occurs whereby language facilitates cognitive development. Limited social, cultural, and educational experiences, therefore, may adversely affect the cognitive skills underlying successful communicative interactions.

> *Cognition provides a substantive base for language acquisition.*

Codification: The importance of codification is to make intent recognizable (Grice, 1975; Sperber & Wilson, 1986). Many deaf individuals use a manually coded language to communicate. Paul and Jackson (1993) reported, "It is important to emphasize that ASL differs from English in grammar and form (sign versus speech)" (p. 47). A deaf person, therefore, may not effectively recognize the intent of a communicated message unless the message is transmitted in either a manual or a written medium that is understood by that person.

> *Codification makes intent recognizable.*

Communication: Bruner (1986) said that intent is the irreducible nucleus of language. Nelson (1985) explained, "In short, the personal and social world is inherently complex and interactive. More importantly, human action is intentional and thus demands interpretation" (p. 37). It is patently obvious that the communication methods differ for

> *Intent is the essence of communication.*

individuals from the Deaf community and those from hearing society. Many deaf individuals use ASL, which is a visual/gestural language, to communicate with one another. Hearing individuals use an aural/oral language system that is based on CCCE. However, the purpose behind communicative interactions, that is, the desire to convey the intent of the message, may be comparable for both deaf and hearing individuals. To say it differently, intent is the essence of communication, regardless of modality. If there is sufficient need for a deaf person and a hearing person to communicate, then a message is likely to be transmitted.

Grossman (1995), however, reported that many aspects of nonverbal communication result in miscommunications across cultures. ASL's grammar and linguistic structure are different from English, and most hearing people do not understand ASL. Also, the emotional, or affective, aspects of ASL can cause communication difficulties.

Expression (Affective): The transmission of emotional meaning is an important aspect of every communicative interaction. It is fraught with problems for both deaf and hearing individuals. A person's mental state is conveyed through facial expression, posture, and, for the hearing culture, through the emotion of voice (Bloom & Beckwith, 1988). Davitz (1966) stated, "A deaf person obviously cannot be very sensitive to vocal expressions simply because he cannot hear the auditory cues involved, but extremely high auditory acuity does not in itself guarantee emotional sensitivity" (p. 473).

> *Expression (affect) is the feeling that is conveyed with a message.*

The hearing person must learn the metalinguistic aspects of ASL, or some miscommunications are likely to occur. Muma (1998) said that "metalinguistic skills are the abilities to reflect on the nature of language" (p. 104). These skills are acquired over varied experiences with language before they become practicable. For example, the subtle nuances of nonmanual cues requiring the use of body language are very sophisticated, and even practiced ASL users may have difficulty interpreting them appropriately (Vernon & Andrews, 1990).

> *Metalinguistic awareness is another aspect of language.*

So how do individuals from Deaf and hearing communities communicate more effectively? Of course, the preferred method is to have a qualified interpreter available who can provide accurate and efficient interpersonal communicative interactions. However, since a qualified

> *When two individuals do not share the same communicative systems (ASL & SAE), it becomes necessary for both to actively negotiate messages.*

interpreter is not always available, it may be necessary for the hearing individual to learn ASL or some other manual language system. The deaf person should use speech reading and/or contextual cues to compensate for the hearing individual's deficient ASL skills. The communication process also can be augmented with writing and verbal communication. This allows for the intent of the message to be recognized.

Nelson (1996) defined the situated mind as the product of an individual's biological, cognitive, linguistic, social, cultural, and emotional circumstances. Bruner (1986) suggested that possible worlds are the end result of learning via one's experiential, social, cultural, and emotional worlds. Both the situated mind and possible worlds are enhanced by linguistic experience.

> *The possible world for one individual is not likely to be the same for another.*

Since language mediates an individual's world (Nelson, 1996), it is important to realize that there may be differences in the situated minds of the communicators. What is possible for one person may not be possible for another due to differences in their experiential, social, cultural, and emotional bases. In understanding the cognitive socialization, or CCCE, approach to language, deaf individuals and hearing persons should strive to meet at least halfway to communicate more effectively with one another.

No two deaf or hard of hearing children are alike. To understand the needs of a particular child, it is necessary to understand the cognitive, linguistic, social, emotional, and cultural contexts within which that child was raised and is functioning. Additionally, many other influences play significant roles; these influences include: the child's nature, potential, temperament, family, social environment, economic opportunities, opportunities for experiential and incidental learning, and the family's response to a hearing loss, not to mention the degree and nature of that hearing loss.

Assessment processes and procedures as well as treatment and instructional practices must account for the uniqueness of each child. The cognition, codification, communication, and expression (CCCE) model may provide more viable understandings for rendering appropriate education to individuals who are deaf or hard of hearing.

— Chapter 7 —

Deaf Education:
Heterogeneity and the CCCE Model

Susan R. Easterbrooks, Ed.D.
Georgia State University

At the 26th annual conference of the Association of College Educators–Deaf/Hard of Hearing (ACE/HH), Muma and Teller (2000) outlined forty different issues, including the centrality of intent, related to the cognitive-socialization perspective on language acquisition that may have an impact on deaf education. Also on the list of issues are heterogeneity and the CCCE model. The complete list of the forty issues appears in Appendix B. The purpose of this chapter is to discuss these issues and heterogeneity as they pertain to deaf education. The following issues are discussed:

> *The deaf and hard of hearing populations are heterogeneous.*

- heterogeneity in the deaf and hard of hearing populations
- elevance of the cognitive socialization perspective to heterogeneity
- interrelationships among heterogeneity, cognitive-socialization, and the CCCE model

Deaf and Hard of Hearing Populations: Heterogeneity

With the advent of P.L. 94-142 and its update P.L. 105-17, the **Individuals with Disabilities Education Act** of 1997, the field of special education identified itself as rendering appropriate services to meet the needs of each individual. Notions of "the handicapped," "the retarded," and "the deaf" were replaced by concerns for "persons who were" handicapped or "who had" retardation or "who were" deaf. While this change

Services in deaf education seem to reflect the homogeneity assumption.

in terminology was well intended, in application, many in education still treat students with disabilities as a homogeneous group. The underlying assumption is that a group of students who are deaf or hard of hearing is composed of individuals with homogeneous difficulties. One needs only to look at the lists of approved modifications that are passed around in individualized educational plan (IEP) meeting after IEP meeting to see that, while students may be identified and labeled based on their differences, they are still educated in similar manners, with similar curricula, and with similar modifications. Such practices underscore the homogeneity assumption. Lieberman (2001) stated:

> Children with disabilities are entitled—no, are practically required—to have the same education as every other child, regardless of whether or not that education is of high quality or is appropriate for a child with a disability . . . . Having the right to fail in regular education is no entitlement. (p. 60)

If a situation is inappropriate for special education, it may be questionable for students who are deaf and hard of hearing.

Sources of Misunderstanding of the Deaf and Hard of Hearing Populations

In its report on the state of deaf education, the **Commission on Education of the Deaf** (Bowe, 1988) pointed out that there is little recognition of the spectrum of needs of individuals who are referred to as

The view that any progress with deaf and hard of hearing students is good progress carries the implicit assumption of homogeneity.

"deaf" and "hard of hearing" or of the fact that these needs change over time. Easterbrooks (1999) further identified issues associated with the attitude that any progress noted in a child with a hearing loss should be cause for celebration. The mistaken perception on the part of many individuals, both inside and outside the field, that any progress is good progress, grossly underestimates the potential of each individual and patently limits progress. This misguided position results in many laypersons remarking that a child is doing well "for a deaf child." It is also solid evidence that the rendered services lack theoretical justification. Some of the factors that lead to misperception are:

- Limited experience with a variety of individuals with hearing losses, causing some to think that all students who are deaf or hard of hearing have the same patterns of learning and potential and resulting in the limited progress of some being viewed as the norm. (For example, a school's only experience has been with Sally, who has intellectual limitations in addition to her hearing loss. Upon Johnny's entrance into the school, they view his potential from their perspective of Sally, even though Johnny has average intelligence.)

- Insufficient or poor early intervention, which results in limited potential (i.e., those students who have not had early intervention and whose potential has been limited are viewed from the same perspective as those who have had early intervention).

- Lack of training and experience on the part of regular education administrators, who are often overwhelmed with the daily management of children, resulting in little time to attend to individual needs.

> *Limited experience with deaf and hard of hearing individuals, inappropriate intervention, and administrator ignorance may all foster the homogeneity assumption.*

- Few children with hearing losses in many public schools, which makes it fiscally impossible to provide the variety of support needed.

- A breakdown in appropriate administrative support from regular education administrators who are confused by some dissention within the field of deaf education itself. (For example, when two deaf educators argue over the correct way to serve one child, the regular education administrator is left in the position of making a decision based on his or her own perspective.)

> *Low incidence of deaf or hard of hearing individuals may preclude appropriate services.*

> *A breakdown in administrative support may be detrimental to appropriate services.*

Stereotypic views of deafness or hard of hearing in general education may be detrimental.

- Antiquated and unchanged perceptions and stereotypes on the part of the general public at large, and the general teaching pool in particular. (For example, many laypersons still use the term "deaf and dumb" and view children with hearing losses in this manner.)

Unwillingness of school systems to cooperate with each other may contribute to poor services.

- Unwillingness of some school systems to think "outside the box" and to cross system lines in search of services. (For example, two students in school system A and two students in school system B are both offered inadequate services because the two systems choose not to share the services of a qualified teacher).

Much needs to be done to inform the education field of the heterogeneous nature of the population, but this cannot be done without first addressing gross misconceptions about what is and is not good enough "for a deaf child."

Contributing to a pervasive mood of limited expectations is the continued reference to limited reading skills of graduates who are deaf and hard of hearing. According to a nationwide study of reading data (Center for Assessment and Demographic Studies, 1991), typical 18- and 19-year-

Although the hard of hearing may average at the fourth grade level in reading, the general public does not do much better.

old deaf students are reading at levels similar to their 9- to 10-year-old hearing peers, or at somewhere around a late third to early fourth grade level. Although on the surface this may seem dismal, deaf and hard of hearing students aren't the only ones having difficulty learning to read. According to the National Institute for Literacy (Kirsch, Jungeblut, Jenkins, & Kolstad, 1993), 21–23% of American adults with normal hearing cannot read well enough to fill out an application, read a food label, or read a simple story to a child. An additional 25–28% can find individual words and compare and contrast them but cannot problem-solve, cannot integrate information requiring two or more sequential operations, and require help from friends and family members in dealing with everyday literacy requirements. This means that as much as 50% of the adult population may struggle with English literacy (Note: These numbers include that segment of the population newly arrived to the United States, who are in various stages of learning English). If lack of hearing were the only factor in learning to read, then all hearing people would be good readers, but this is simply not the case, and when seen in the light of national statistics, the results for students with hearing losses do not seem quite so startling. The long-reported fact that deaf and hard of hearing students on average graduate with about a fourth grade reading level is, sadly, consistent with the above findings on hearing adults. On the other hand, if fourth grade is the average, then half read below and half read above that level. This means that at least half, if not more, of the deaf and hard of hearing population is able to read well enough to handle sequential information, to fill out forms, and to get by on a daily basis without assistance.

> *The average reading level for the hard of hearing means that some of these individuals do better than the average.*

By viewing the population of students with hearing losses as if they were a homogeneous group, misinterpretation of the numbers are perpetuated. These misinterpretations lead some to think that all children with hearing losses learn in the same manner and face the same fate (i.e., the often repeated and incorrect notion that deaf children cannot read beyond a fourth grade level). Just ask the many adults who are deaf and who graduated from high school with reading skills sufficient to pass them through standard exit examinations if all students with hearing losses are alike.

> *The homogeneity assumption leads to misinterpretation of various data.*

Characteristics of Heterogeneity

The population of students who are deaf and hard of hearing evidences traits and characteristics that lie along multiple continua. Easterbrooks and Baker (2001) identified at least eleven different ways in which the degree of loss interacted with family background and early experiences. Children with hearing losses are not simply either deaf or hard of hearing, either smart or of limited intellect, or either anything as opposed to the other; rather, they are the sum total of points along many different continua, and each trait makes its own unique contribution to a sense of who that child is.

> *Individuals with hearing loss may vary in at least eleven different ways from each other.*

Just as a finely tuned orchestra plays music one way and then another, the myriad tones, undertones, and beats of heterogeneity come together to form the tune that is each child.

Traditionally, individual traits and characteristics are viewed from several contexts: physical, cognitive, emotional, and social-experiential. Physically, children who are deaf or hard of hearing differ based on the following traits, among others:

> *Ways that individuals may differ physically*

- gender
- degree of hearing loss
- type of hearing loss
- relative usefulness of medical and technical applications to enhance physical traits
- presence or absence of physical disorders such as temporary or chronic illness, limited mobility, or any other physical challenge that impacts the population at large

Cognitively, children who are deaf or hard of hearing differ based on such traits as:

- global, genetically predetermined intellectual potential, from severe retardation to giftedness

> *Ways that individuals may differ cognitively*

- specific neurological and neurochemically based learning differences such as learning disabilities and attention deficient hyperactivity disorder (ADHD)
- acquired neurological challenges due to external factors such as fetal exposure to alcohol and drugs, exposure to toxic drugs, chemicals or environmental pollutants, or acquired traumatic brain injury, any of which may have a mild to profound or a specific to diffuse impact

Emotionally, children who are deaf and hard of hearing vary on such traits as:

- native temperament

> *Ways that individuals may differ emotionally*

- relative status within a family such as birth order, number of children, and whether or not children are cherished
- presence or absence of neurochemically based challenges such as obsessive compulsive disorde (OCD), childhood schizophrenia, or Tourette Syndrome

- the availability of consistent, emotionally available and nurturing parents or caregivers
- the ease with which the child has his needs met, which impacts his perception of the world as a trustworthy or hostile place

Socially and experientially, children who are deaf and hard of hearing vary on such traits as:

- family acceptance of a hearing loss, including the presence or absence of other deaf or hard of hearing family members
- the language of the home, whether spoken or signed, English or ASL, English or another spoken language
- accessibility to a shared communication system within the family
- accessibility to a shared communication system with peers

> *Ways that individuals may differ socially and experientially*

- the relative importance and support the family places on educational attainment, such as reading to the child or sending the child to school consistently
- the relative financial ability to expose the child to the larger world around him

The undeniable message, then, is that when deaf or hard of hearing students are grouped on the basis of one variable, the other variables introduce such diversity that the grouping is undone.

In other words, the heterogeneous nature of the deaf and hard of hearing population is so pervasive that any effort to view them as alike or to render similar services may be doomed from the outset. With this veritable smorgasbord of characteristics and traits that impact a child's development, it is impossible to expect that there is one way, one treatment, one method, or one technology that could be a panacea available to educators.

> *The deaf and hard of hearing populations are notoriously heterogeneous.*

Basic Premises of Cognitive Socialization

According to the cognitive socialization view, communication is a cognitive-social process (Brown, 1956; Bruner, 1973, 1975, 1981, 1990; Nelson, 1985, 1996; Vygotsky, 1962). Cognitive-socialization theorists

Cognitive growth, including language, occurs in a social nexus.	hold that social interaction is the impetus for learning. "Cognitive growth occurs mainly in a social nexus" (Mandler, 1978, p. 375). **Intent** is regarded as the essence of a message and that intent determines the way in which we converse (Bruner, 1986; Searle, 1992).

Communicative intent (what we want the other person to know or do) influences the words a child chooses, the grammar used to tie words together, and the means (speech or signs) by which intent is conveyed.

The world that makes sense to a child, the **possible world** (Bruner, 1986), is based on the child's past experiences (Lakoff, 1987). Since perception is relative to past experience (Garner, 1966; Glasser, 1998), a child responds to information from the perspective of that child's **situated mind** (Nelson, 1996). Nelson showed that frame of reference is solidly located within a set of cognitive-social-cultural-emotional experiences. Each child's experiences, each nuance ascribed to these experiences by significant people around him (especially caregivers and subsequently peers), and the way that such experiences become labeled for the child (referred to as a dubbing ceremony by Bruner, 1981) provides a fundamental base upon which future communication and learning rest.

One's experiential base comprises that individual's possible worlds.

Rethinking Heterogeneity: The CCCE Model

Muma (1998) and Muma and Teller (2001) delineated the CCCE model as having potentials for understanding the communication development of students who are deaf and hard of hearing. This model views language not from the perspective of modalities (expressive/receptive language) nor form, content, and use, but from the perspective of **cognition, codification, communication,** and **expression** in keeping with speech acts theory (Austin, 1962; Grice, 1975; Searle, 1969, 1983), relevance theory (Sperber & Wilson, 1986), and bootstrapping theory (Gleitman, 1994; Pinker, 1984). **Cognition** pertains to how the mind works, including its ability to categorize, represent, attend, plan and execute its tasks as

The CCCE perspective is compatible with appreciating individual differences.

intended. Memory is a key component of cognition but it is not an entity that can be isolated from an individual's available repertoire (Hudson & Fivush, 1990). One's possible world (Bruner, 1986) and situated

> *Cognition pertains to how the mind works.*

mind (Nelson, 1996) constitute working cognition for an individual whereby experiences contribute to that individual's world knowledge.

Codification pertains to the process of turning intent into a form so that someone else will recognize it; that is, messages are coded in order to make intent recognizable (Grice, 1975; Sperber & Wilson, 1986). There are alternative ways or pathways to code intent (Easterbrooks & Baker, 2001). The important point is that each brain seeks to code (planning and execution) and compre-

> *Codification is the act of coding a message so that intent can be recognized.*

hend codes (construction and utilization) toward making intent recognizable (Clark & Clark, 1977; Grice, 1975; Sperber & Wilson, 1986).

By **communication**, Muma (1998) referred to the pragmatic arena. Citing Bruner (1986) and Searle (1992), he described their strong case for the centrality of intent in all communication as the irreducible nucleus of language. Intent is the purpose for communication, and it is based on both cognition (possible worlds) and social interaction.

> *Communication is the act of rendering intent recognizable within social and cultural constraints.*

Expression, an overlooked component of communication, refers to affect or emotion. It is a key aspect in the expression and recognition of intent. Affect or emotion is conveyed through inflection and tone of voice in spoken English and through facial expression and other body indicators in ASL.

> *Expression is the emotional side of communication.*

Affect, or expression, allows us to express emotional content of communication as well as to capture the listener/watcher's attention (Brown, 1977; Lock, 1978). The expressive-affective component of communication has not received much attention in the deaf education literature.

Cultural Context and the CCCE Model

The CCCE model explains how the child's thinking and communication skills develop within the context of culture, both the cultures of

Social and cultural influences have a leveling effect on learning.

the family and of the broader society, including the Deaf culture. In terms of cognition, the social experiences of a child determine and are determined by how the caregivers in his environment guide early experiences with the world. Categorization, representation, and memory are key cognitive functions that form the early bases of understanding and interaction with the world. Categories of information are highly influenced by the culture of the family and the culture of the larger society. In terms of codification, the language code a family uses has a significant impact on the child. If that code is spoken English, then he will learn one word for a concept. If it is spoken Spanish, then he will learn another. If it is signed English, he may learn one sign for a concept, and if it is ASL, he may learn a different sign. The emphasis a family places on the code governs, to some extent, the nature of communicative development.

Regarding communication, the intent of a message is the central, driving force of that message. It is the basis for communication. Every family has its own unique set of values and beliefs. Initially, micropragmatic skills come from deep personal needs. Rapidly, however, they are modified by the need for acceptance from and identification with the culture of the family and the culture of the broader social world.

The whole communication enterprise centers on intent.

The affective-expressive intent of one's message is also controlled by how one perceives affect-expression (i.e., the emotion one hears or sees in the communication of others) and how these expressions are accepted by others (e.g., whether valued or ridiculed). For example, in some families, pets are viewed as dirty and parasitic, good only for the work they can do, while in other families pets are given the status of a cherished member. These perspectives are conveyed to the child in subtle ways, and the child will maintain these perspectives until his personal experiences and personal choices guide him to modify his position. Words used to represent pets convey these attitudes.

Memories of experiences are coded both verbally and nonverbally. A child hears or sees how others treat animals and hears or sees how others perceive his interactions with pets. For example, a child may learn that it is acceptable to be physically aggressive with animals or may learn that aggression will not be tolerated. A child may learn that it is acceptable to curse an animal, or may learn that cursing is not tolerated. A child may learn that the reaction to an animal's antics result in anger or that they result in compassion. What a child learns is integrally tied to the social fabric of the child's personal, social, cultural, and emotional worlds.

Revisiting Heterogeneity: The CCCE Model

As described earlier, the population of students who are deaf and hard of hearing is heterogeneous rather than homogeneous. One way in which the heterogeneous nature of the population impacts communication development has to do with families themselves. Communication development is a highly personal issue, which is most significantly influenced by the family early on. Subsequently, peer influence plays an increasingly important role. Families of students who are deaf and hard of hearing have a seemingly endless variety of options when learning to communicate with their child. Each family will choose the approach that works best within the context of that family. The number of available technologies increases on a daily basis. Medical options exist today that did not exist for the previous generation. Educational options appear to be endless on the surface, but in reality, they are dictated by the geographical and financial resources of a family. It is a long-held notion in deaf education that parents have educational options. This is true for the educated parent who aggressively seeks services and treatments and/or who has the financial resources to go or move to where services are available. However, this is not an option for many families. Sometimes choices are made by default. Many families have historical, familial, and financial ties to a specific town or region, and if a variety of services are not available in that town or region, the child receives the service, education, treatment, or technology that is available.

> *Family structure and values play significant roles in providing services for deaf and hard of hearing individuals.*

Families vary not only in their responses to a hearing loss but in their very make-up as well. Some families have two parents who work together for the child's development. In some families, parents are at odds over how best to proceed. Other families have only one parent. Still others are foster families. Some families have only one child and can devote full attention to that child's needs. Others have many children, all of whom require attention. Some families have a supportive, extended family and can depend upon extra support to meet the demands of the child and his special needs. Others go it alone, struggling with the challenges of meeting basic needs, let alone the special challenges that accompany a hearing loss. Some families have the beliefs and values assumed to be held by the general American culture. Others hold beliefs and values that the general American culture views as self-oriented or negative. Still other families come from cultures outside the general American culture, and their beliefs and values are more aligned with those of their native culture than those of the general American culture. For example, most people use simple gestures in everyday conversation, yet gestures vary greatly from one culture to another, and it is very easy to make a gesture that a person from another culture views as offensive. Communication can be achieved not only verbally but nonverbally. Nonverbal communication develops within a familial and cultural context just as does verbal communication. In all, these variations underscore the heterogeneous nature of the deaf and hard of hearing population.

> *Clearly, family dynamics contribute to individual differences in the hard of hearing.*

Initially, choices made for children with hearing losses are made within the context of the family. Later, they are made by the culture of the school that the child attends. Schools traditionally base instruction of students with disabilities on the development of an IEP, and IEPs are typically driven by standardized tests. According to Muma and Teller (2001), standardized, normative tests are based on the notion of homogeneity; there is one standard way a child should think, talk, act, or behave at any given point in time. This point of view holds that development adheres to a lock-stepped hierarchy. On the contrary, no two children develop in precisely the same way, at the same pace, or under the exact same circumstances even within the same family.

> *Critical decisions about appropriate services for individuals with a hearing loss begin in the home, and the schools eventually play a role.*

Given that each child with a hearing loss has multiple influences on his development (e.g., family, school, medicine, technology, personality, potential), the idea of *the typical child* is false. Using standardized

> *The notion of a typical child with a hearing loss is false.*

tests upon which comparisons are made, ignores the real, multifaceted, complicated nature of a child and imposes some false notions of "normal."

In 1840, de Tocqueville referred to the unquestioned acceptance of a majority opinion as the "tyranny of the majority" (Nash, 2000), which is the tendency to conform to what is perceived as a majority opinion. Tyranny of the majority has been responsible for negative attitudes toward persons with disabilities for centuries. It is also responsible for burdensome, high-stakes testing which presently has a stranglehold on today's schools. Instead, Muma (1998) and Muma and Teller (2001) recommend that decisions about instructional needs should be based on the following:

> *The tyranny of the majority is detrimental for heterogeneous populations.*

- the individual's repertoire of skills
- progress in acquisition sequences
- available learning strategies, and
- active loci of learning

A child's personal experiences determine the way he understands information. Simply quantifying the number or types of words or structures a child has compared to another child will give the teacher no insight into his understanding of that language. Recall the two perspectives on pets described earlier. If the teacher has one perspective on pets and the student another, they are bound to have conflicts when the teacher tries to build new information on her perspective rather than the child's. True understanding of a child's repertoire of skills can come only from spending time with that child, getting to know him. That is dependent upon engaging the child in communication. Clarke-Stewart (1973) found that the amount of child-directed speech by mothers was highly correlated with later linguistic competence of the child. Hart and Risley (1995) studied the quality and quantity of communicative interactions between 42 hearing children and their parents and found that the amount of communicative interaction was the best predictor of later language and reading success, no matter what the family's circumstances were. Sadly, many teachers of the deaf do not engage children with hearing losses in sufficient conversational time,

> *Teachers should engage individuals with hearing loss in actual social commerce rather than rely on prepackaged materials.*

either to forge the social bonds that result in true understanding of a child or to get sufficient information about a child's current repertoire of skills. Knowledge of what a child understands, how he is progressing, what strategies he is using to communicate and to learn, and what skills are most likely to develop next (the low-hanging fruit, most readily picked) are more important when determining effective and efficient instruction in communication.

———=»·0·«=———

Many substantive developments have occurred in the last decade (Cloud & Muma, 1999) that require substantive shifts from the traditional generation to the new cognitive socialization generation. These shifts are underscored by the heterogeneous nature of clinical populations. Accordingly, teachers of the deaf and hard of hearing should have a rationale for rendering services that have continuity with these developments.

———=»·0·«=———

Chapter 8

Rationale:
Something Old, Something New

John R. Muma, Ph.D.
University of Southern Mississippi

Fran Hagstrom, Ph.D.
University of Arkansas

Why do deaf education services differ from one teacher to another? Assuming that the teachers are adequately trained and certified, the differences are likely to be due to different philosophical views and theoretical perspectives. Accordingly, clinicians may have different rationales or positions as to why clinical services are rendered in particular ways.

Deaf education teachers differ because of varied philosophical views.

Teachers who follow a behavioristic view and the reinforcement theory (Fey, 1986; Paul, 1995) render services that are quite different from those who follow a constructionistic view (Bruner, 1986) and relevance theory (Sperber & Wilson, 1986). The former might be regarded as following a traditional generation whereas the latter is more aligned with the contemporary scholarly literature constituting the new cognitive socialization generation. Figure 8.1 (page 104) contrasts the old traditional and new cognitive socialization generations.

The behaviorist view is a traditional view.

The traditional approach in deaf education was oriented on the modality model of language. This model was proposed by Osgood (1957). It held that there were crucial differences between the expressive and receptive modalities and between the spoken and written

The modality view is a traditional view.

modalities. Accordingly, many tests and intervention programs in deaf education have been oriented on modalities such as expressive (speaking, writing) and receptive (listening, reading).

Traditional Approach: Reinforcement
- Modality orientation
- Quantification: Frequency based (percentage)
- Normative tests: Questionable construct validity
- Reinforcement

New Approach: Cognitive Socialization
- CCCE orientation
- Contextual evidence
- Descriptive evidence: repertoire, acquisition sequences, strategies of learning, and active loci of learning
- Intent replacing reinforcement

Figure 8.1. Comparisons between the traditional and cognitive socialization generations.

Although there are differences between modalities, these differences are relatively minor when compared to the core issues of language that are common to all modalities. The new generation addresses the language core rather than the modalities and is more in accordance with the contemporary cognitive socialization literature. To underscore this shift, it should be recognized that none of the major language scholars such as Bloom, Brown, Bruner, Cazden, Chomsky, Mandler, Nelson, Pinker, Searle, Sperber, and Wilson have adopted the modality model whereas they do address the core issues discussed below. Indeed, the final death-knell for the modality model appeared in Clark and Clark (1977), in which modality information was shown to be purged before the essential cognitive activity for information processing takes place.

The modality view misses the core language issues.

The traditional approach evidences a reliance on **quantification** rather than a description of available verbal repertoires. In the tradition of the tired old notion of habit strength, the traditional approach counts frequencies of behavior and converts these frequencies into percentages as presumed evidence of learning. Perhaps it is useful to turn to a quote from Cazden (1988, p. 281) that not only indicates that frequency but also reinforcement provide inappropriate accounts of language acquisition: "To put the conclusions bluntly: Reinforcement did not exist, frequency did not correlate. . . ."

> *Frequencies of behavior is a traditional view.*

The contemporary view is that lexical variation provides more appropriate evidence of language acquisition than frequency per se (Bloom, Rispoli, Gartner, & Hafitz, 1989). Moreover, it is more appropriate to ascertain an individual's available repertoire or range of linguistic skills than merely count instances (Ninio, Snow, Pan, & Rollins, 1994). For example, it is more useful to ascertain alternative structural variations available to an individual for the subject nominal system than to merely count that that individual used a particular structure a given number of times. Frequency can be useful when it is coupled with lexical variation to provide evidence of consolidation or productivity (Ingram, 1989; Muma, 1986, 1998).

> *Lexical variation has replaced frequencies of behavior.*

The conversion of frequency to percentage is a common practice in the traditional approach. When instances of behavior are less than 100, this conversion creates an illusion by virtue of data inflation. For example, when an individual has ten of twenty instances of correct tense marking, that individual is said to have 50% correct. But, the use of percentage in this way creates a subtle illusion because the data were inflated by a factor of five (5 X 20 = 100). Furthermore, when such percentages are compared before and after intervention as presumed evidence of accountability or efficacy, a two-faced illusion occurs because these comparisons often use different databases, thereby creating disproportionate inflations of the data. The traditional generation has been silent about such problems.

> *The conversion of frequencies of behavior to percentages creates illusions.*

The following are examples of this problem. Rice, Haney, and Wexler (1989) provided the following statement: "The positive history findings are as follows for the 31 proband families: (a) 58.1%, (b) 35.5%, (c) 64.5%, and for the 67 control families, (a) 19.4%, (b) 22.4%, (c) 37.3%." Another example is the set of figures (1–8) on page 1421 in Rice, Wexler, and Hershberger (1998).

The traditional approaches have placed inordinate reliance on normative tests in conducting language assessment. This has created three major problems. First, there is a misunderstanding in the clinical fields regarding the presumed need for normative tests. The widespread belief is that standardized assessment must be achieved by the use of normative tests. Indeed, most state Offices of Special Education provide lists of recommended language tests for standardized assessment. However, the national Office of Special Education issued an official policy statement for standardized assessment in accordance with P.L. 94-142 (Martin, 1980). The statement reads, "The basis for that judgment is the child's performance on formal and/or informal measures of linguistic competence and performance, rather than heavy reliance on the results of academic achievement testing." This judgment is for eligibility for special education services. Thus, standardized assessment may be achieved with formal and/or informal assessments.

> *Standardized assessment may be achieved with formal and/or informal measures.*

Second, there is a serious problem with the use of formal language tests in the clinical fields. It is that these tests are notoriously weak because of their of lack construct validity. Muma (forthcoming) has recently completed a comprehensive review of the extent to which about twenty widely used language tests meet the contemporary criteria for construct validity (Messick, 1980, 1989, 1995). Muma and Brannon (1986) surveyed the ten most widely used language tests in the clinical fields and found that none meet the contemporary criteria for construct validity. Most claimed construct validity from an empirical standpoint. However, none of these tests were based on bona fide language theories. Yet, the contemporary theory of construct validity calls for theory-based assessments because theories provide appropriate understandings of a given domain. This circumstance means that these tests merely have norms that sanction the test developers' biases rather

> *Language tests are notoriously weak in meeting the current standards for construct validity.*

than tests that have substantive continuity with the relevant literature. This circumstance continues today and probably accounts for why about 50% of the clinicians in the field are dissatisfied with the available tests (Huang, Hopkins, & Nippold, 1997).

Perhaps it is useful to turn to the major scholars in the field of test and measurement. *"All measurement should be construct referenced"* (Messick, 1975, p. 957). *"All* validity is at its base some form of construct validity. . . .It *is* the basic meaning of validity"* (Guion, 1977, p. 410). Moreover, construct validity is the appropriate interpretation of available evidence as defined by the relevant theoretical perspectives. This means that raw empirical attempts to define construct validity by virtue of various factor analytic procedures still need to be grounded on a theory for appropriate interpretation.

> *All measurement should be construct based.*

Third, standardized descriptive procedures issuing from the contemporary scholarly literature in language acquisition provide useful assessment procedures. Indeed, these procedures are more useful than test scores for the simple reason that they deal with spontaneous speech that constitutes prima facie evidence of what an individual can do. Said differently, what an individual does in actual social commerce provides prima facie evidence of what that individual can do. Therefore, rather than test scores (contrived performance of questionable relevance), it is more appropriate to ascertain verbal abilities based on what an individual does in actual social commerce. With such evidence, it is possible to ascertain an individual's available repertoire (Ninio, Snow, Pan, & Rollins, 1994), progress in acquisition sequences (Brown, 1973), alternative learning strategies (Goldfield & Snow, 2001), and active loci of learning (Muma, 1983, 1986, 1998).

> *Prima facie evidence is what an individual does in actual social commerce.*

For example, the PPVT-III is widely used in special education as presumed evidence of vocabulary and even receptive language and intelligence. However, for over a decade, it has been known that this test misses the three most important issues of vocabulary or word knowledge. It misses intentional meaning because it only deals with elicited meaning. It misses referential meaning because there are no opportunities to ascertain one word/many referents and one referent/many words. It misses combinatorial meaning because there is no opportunity to ascertain an

The PPVT-III misses three crucial issues of vocabulary.

individual's abilities to use various words in combination with other words. Indeed, if the literature on word acquisition is considered (Kuczaj & Barrett, 1986), the PPVT-III could be regarded as somewhat of an embarrassment as a presumed test of vocabulary. Yet, the clinical fields remain undaunted and continue to use this test to assess vocabulary, receptive language, and even intelligence. In contrast, the literature on word learning provides many viable options for assessing what an individual can do (Kuczaj & Barrett).

The traditional clinical approach evidences a reliance on reinforcement. However, the scholarly literature over the past three decades has

Reinforcement does not provide a viable account of language acquisition.

indicated that behaviorism and reinforcement provide unsatisfactory perspectives (Bruner, 1978; Chomsky, 1968). The following quote conveys the traditional view: "There is absolutely no question that operant procedures are effective in getting children to produce new utterances that are more complex in structure than utterances produced by those same children prior to intervention" (Fey, 1986, p. 144).

In contrast, the contemporary scholarly view disavowed the appro-

The absurdity of reinforcement is that it does not deal with internal mental states.

priateness of reinforcement as a viable account of language acquisition. "Models of language acquisition built explicitly on assumptions of positive and negative reinforcement are no longer acceptable" (Nelson, 1985, p. 33). Referring to an individual's ability to deduce grammatical rules, Macken (1987, p. 380) indicated that this ability is "*quite* unlike an empiricist reinforcement schedule." Finally, Searle (1992, p. 35) states, "The absurdity of behaviorism lies in the fact that it denies the existence of any mental states."

New Model: Cognitive Socialization

Over the past three decades or so, major developments (approximately forty; see Appendix B) have occurred that raise serious questions about the adequacy of the traditional clinical model. Inasmuch as the American Speech-Language-Hearing Association Code of Ethics holds that the client's welfare should be first and foremost and the federal legislation mandates that clients are entitled to the most appropriate services, it behooves the clinical fields to make concerted efforts to become re-aligned to the available scholarly literature. Toward this end, the cognitive socialization field offers many new issues for rendering appropriate services, thereby establishing a new model.

> *The cognitive socialization literature provides substantive issues for appropriate services.*

The new model is based on the field of cognitive socialization (Brown, 1956, 1986), which is an expanded orientation from what was previously known as psycholinguistics. In keeping with many new developments in the scholarly literature, the new clinical model departs considerably from the traditional clinical model.

Rather than the traditional modality model, the new model is oriented on the CCCE core issues of language. These issues are: cognition, codification, communication, and expression. "We offer a theory of language development which integrates the social interaction, cognitive, and linguistic theories" (Bloom, Beckwith, Capatides, & Hafitz, 1988, p. 103). ". . . language development interacts with developments in cognition and in social-emotional functioning" (Ely, 1997, p. 398). "Language is seen then as a cognitive-communicative invention" (Nelson, 1996, p. 54). It should be stressed that the notion of expression in this context does not refer to the expressive modalities; rather, it refers to the affective or emotional aspect of language.

> *Cognitive socialization is based on the core CCCE issues of language.*

Muma (1998) has identified thirteen major developments in **cognition** that are directly relevant to language acquisition. For example, Bruner's (1986) notion of possible worlds and Nelson's (1996) notion of situated mind coupled with the current view that cognitive development occurs in a social nexus (Mandler, 1979; Rogoff, 1990; Wertsch, 1991) make it abundantly clear that it is necessary to expand and vary a child's experiential and social worlds toward establishing a viable cognitive substrata for language acquisition. This is especially urgent for pregrammatical children (before a child can construct varied subject-verb-object structures). The developments pertaining to the centrality of intent (Bruner, 1986), content in the

> *Cognitive socialization has yielded thirteen new issues in cognition.*

service of intent (Sperber & Wilson, 1986), the shift from procedural to semantic knowledge with the assistance of mimesis (Nelson, 1996), schemata (Lakoff, 1987), and representation (Mandler, 1983) constitute major advancements in understanding the cognitive bases of language. Indeed, these and other issues provide a model of the cognitive bases of language (Muma, 1998). All of these issues are beyond the purview of the traditional clinical model.

The current literature indicates that it is desirable to extend the meaning of language across a wide range of formal coding mechanisms— linguistic, pragmatic, gestural, postural, and so on.

> *Cognitive socialization provides a broader view of language.*

The linguistic domain (semantic, syntactic, phonological) is the most elaborate, to be sure, but issues such as shared reference, two-person sentences, line-of-regard, the communicative point, displayed referents, and other performatives and contexts constitute crucially important insights into the beginning of language acquisition, and therefore they contribute to a new clinical approach. Thus, **codification** is more encompassing than the traditional views of language.

Communication refers to the use of language in social commerce. This is the pragmatic area. The two crucial issues for communication are the centrality of intent and context. "Describing a

> *The two crucial issues for communication are intent and context.*

speaker's repertoires of communicative intents and rules for expressing those intents is crucial to any complete description of the language capacity" (Ninio, Snow, Pan, & Rollins, 1994, p. 157). The essential purpose of communication is to make intent recognizable (Grice, 1975; Sperber & Wilson, 1986). While the traditional model has acknowledged intent, it has been silent about the centrality of intent.

As for context, Bruner (1981, p. 172) indicated, "Context is all." Nelson (1985) delineated twelve different kinds of contexts that con-

> *Context is all.*

tribute to language acquisition. While the traditional approach has acknowledged context, it only refers to context in a vague and abject manner.

The notion of **expression** in CCCE refers to the affective or emotional aspect of language acquisition. Except for the role of neutral affect in word acquisition (Bloom, Beckwith, Capatides, & Hafitz, 1988), very little research has been done on the role of affect. "The great chasm to be bridged in both speculations on the evolution of language and those on its development is that between affective and referential communication" (Lock, 1978, p. 8). Given this disparity, it

> *Expression pertains to feelings or emotion.*

is incumbent on the field of special education to turn to the attachment theory (Ainsworth, 1973; Bowlby, 1973) as an appropriate perspective for appreciating emotional development during the early language acquisition years. Muma (1981) has developed an assessment procedure based on this literature.

Needless to say, teachers oriented on the traditional clinical approach may want to become oriented on the new cognitive socialization approach. In so doing, they would become more aligned with the current scholarly literature.

Contextual evidence coupled with descriptive evidence derived from actual social commerce provides prima facie evidence of what an individual can do. Such evidence opens the door to several major new perspectives that heretofore were not considered in the traditional approach. For example, descriptive evidence provides a means of ascertaining an individual's repertoire of various semantic skills (basic propositions, Greenfield & Smith, 1976), syntactic (with lexical variation, Bloom, Rispoli, Gartner, & Hafitz, 1989), phonological (phonological processes, Vihman & Greenlee, 1987; homonymy, Priestley, 1980; phonological avoidance, Schwartz & Leonard, 1982), and pragmatic skills (Grice, 1975; anaphora and deic-

> *Descriptive evidence offers opportunities to ascertain an individual's repertoires, progress in sequences, strategies, and active loci of learning.*

tic reference, Lust, 1986a, b). No tests can ascertain repertoires of these skills. Suffice to say the traditional approach has missed a great deal.

Finally, the new approach is based on the centrality of intent that was mentioned above. To reiterate, the purpose of communication is to make intent recognizable. Clinical services that are based on intent have effectively replaced reinforcement as a more viable account of language acquisition. Interestingly, the longstanding problem for

> *The crucial issue for language is intent.*

reinforcement was that while individuals may function relatively well in a clinical setting, they would typically evidence a lack of carryover or generalization outside of the clinical setting. The cognitive socialization approach offers a viable solution to this problem. The focus on intent typically results in children performing noticeably better at home and in their general ecology *before* evidencing improvements in the clinic. That is, it is not unusual to have mothers and/or teachers report that their children evidenced noticeable improvements before they did so in the clinic. Thus, an intent-oriented intervention has been shown to be more effective than reinforcement. It is our experience that mothers who have had their children in both the traditional reinforcement approach and the new approach that focuses on intent have commented that they and their children prefer the new approach much more.

Heterogeneity

Special education has a special problem. It is the heterogeneous nature of clinical populations. Strangely, the reliance on normative tests with their homogeneity assumption and treatment comparisons as presumed evidence of effectiveness with their assumption of homogeneity also become undermined by the heterogeneous nature of clinical populations. Another misguided notion that is undone by heterogeneity is exemplified by various efforts to define specific language impairment as a phenotype (Tager-Flusberg & Cooper, 2000). In short, heterogeneity haunts the clinical fields to the core (Muma, 1998). With these serious limitations, an empirical justification or rationale is evidently misguided. Rather, a rationale should be conceptual in nature, predicated on appropriate philosophical views and theoretical perspectives.

> *Heterogeneity is at the heart of clinical fields.*

Rationale

> *Deaf education teachers should know which philosophical views underwrite their teaching rationales.*

Teachers in deaf education should be able to state specific philosophical views and theoretical perspectives that predicate particular educational services. These views and perspectives constitute a rationale for rendering services in particular ways. Given the traditional and new approaches, teachers would have different rationales or justifications for rendering services in particular ways.

The new cognitive socialization approach is based on several complementary philosophical views and theoretical perspectives. Searle (1992) critiqued the following philosophical views of language and cognition: behaviorism, monism, dualism, materialism, functionalism, and constructionism. Lakoff (1987) showed that objectivity was a myth. Bruner (1978) indicated that positivism (reinforcement theory) merely yielded "corrosive dogmatism" (p. viii) in language acquisition accounts. The bottom line of these various considerations is that constructionism and functionalism provide the most coherent accounts, especially the former. Teachers should strive to orient their rationales on constructionism and possibly functionalism as philosophical bases issuing from the cognitive socialization literature.

> *Constructionism has surpassed behaviorism as a more appropriate philosophical view.*

The key issue for constructionism is that a client is an active processor of information. Consequently, the crucial roles of a clinician are to describe (Muma, 1978, 1986, 1998):

a. what an individual can do (repertoire)
b. what progress the individual has made in acquisition sequences
c. what strategies of learning are available to the individual
d. what the individual's active loci of learning are

> *The key issue for constructionism is that an individual is an active processor of information.*

Notice that traditional special education has been silent about not only these four issues but what philosophical views predicate its services. Typically, when the issue of philosophical views (and theoretical perspectives) is raised, special education is either dumbfounded or appeals to eclecticism, which is tantamount to licensing dogma.

Perera (1994), the editor of the *Journal of Child Language*, perhaps the most highly revered journal in language acquisition, identified the five most influential theories of language acquisition over the previous twenty-five years. These were:

a. government binding or parameter setting (Atkinson, 1992; Chomsky, 1982; Lightfoot, 1989)
b. modularity (Fodor, 1983)
c. speech acts or relevance (Grice, 1975; Sperber & Wilson, 1986)

> *Reinforcement was not one of the most influential theories of language acquisition over the previous four decades.*

d. bootstrapping (Bruner, 1981; Gleitman, 1994; Gleitman, Gleitman, Landau, & Wanner, 988; Grimshaw, 1981; Pinker, 1984, 1987)

e. connectionism or parallel distributed processing (McClelland & Rumelhart, 1986)

Notice that reinforcement theory was not on the list. Indeed, reinforcement theory has several major problems (Kohn, 1993; Searle, 1992).

From the perspective of establishing a rationale, speech acts or relevance theories and the bootstrapping theories are promising candidates simply because they have continuity with constructionsm and because they offer substantive issues that extend beyond the narrow linguistic domain per se to the broader communicative domain. Furthermore, CCCE is implicit, if not explicit, in these theories.

Speech acts and relevance theories provide useful understandings for deaf education because they are oriented on CCCE with the centrality of intent. These theories have four basic dimensions: intent, content (implicit and explicit), the linguistic nature of a message, and the effects of a message on a listener. Needless to say, it behooves clinicians to address each of these issues.

> *Speech acts and relevance theories are compatible with constructionism.*

Bootstrapping theories are also useful to deaf education because they focus on the various roles of different kinds of context in language acquisition. Teachers should vary contexts as a way of fostering and documenting language acquisition.

> *Bootstrapping theories address various kinds of contexts that support language acquisition.*

Given these issues, views, and perspectives, teachers are in a position to know and state their rationales for rendering educational services in particular ways. With these rationales, teachers may ascertain the degree to which they are aligned with the relevant scholarly literature.

Conscientious Clinician (CC) or Careless Clinician (cc)

Conscientious clinicians (CC) or teachers hold that their students' welfare is first and foremost. Thus, these teachers are interested in the contemporary literature with its philosophical views and theoretical perspectives simply because these views and perspectives define rationales for appropriate services.

In contrast, teachers who do not care about providing appropriate services are **careless clinicians (cc) or teachers** with regard to philosophical views and theoretical perspectives. They take this view: "Don't give me theory. Just tell me what to do." Because the role of theory is to provide understandings, teachers who expressly do not want theoretical perspectives have taken the stance that they do not care about understanding their students and their services. Thus, these teachers have become technicians who place themselves ahead of their students.

Teachers have a choice as to whether they become conscientious (CC) or careless (cc). Those who are conscientious strive to keep abreast of new developments in the contemporary literature. Approximately forty major new developments have occurred in the scholarly literature over the past two decades (Cloud & Muma, 1999). These developments offer many improvements over the traditional views and practices. By incorporating these developments into services, teachers place their students' welfare first and foremost.

> *Conscientious clinicians or teachers are interested in the contemporary literature because they place their client's welfare first and foremost.*

> *Careless clinicians or teachers are not interested in philosophical views or theoretical perspectives.*

> *Deaf education teachers have a choice as to whether they want to be conscientious or careless.*

Assessments well done, grounded on appropriate philosophical views and theoretical perspectives, provide teachers of the deaf and hard of hearing with useful and practical perspectives. Grammatical assessments should deal with the basic grammatical systems: subject nominal, object nominal, auxiliary, verbal, and grammatical operations. Such assessments should address an individual's available repertoire, progress in acquisition sequences, strategies of learning, and active loci of learning; they also should incorporate appropriate attribution criteria. Such evidence would greatly advance the services rendered to deaf and hard of hearing individuals.

— Chapter 9 —

Grammatical Assessment: Theory Predicates Practice

John R. Muma, Ph.D.
University of Southern Mississippi

Alfred H. White, Jr., Ph.D.
Texas Woman's University

"An assessment well done is a treatment half begun" (Prutting, Epstein, Beckman, Dias, & Gao, 1989, p. 12). The purpose of this chapter is to provide "assessments well done." In doing so, it will become abundantly clear that theories provide an underlying conceptual basis—rationale—for appropriate grammatical assessment. By doing so, deaf education becomes aligned with the scholarly literature thereby rendering appropriate assessment. Thus, theoretical perspectives make grammatical assessment practical and achieve a scholarly stance.

> *Theoretical perspectives make assessment practical and achieve scholarship.*

Such endeavors provide teachers of the deaf and hard of hearing useful and practical ways of assessing language. It is *useful* because it provides valid evidence of what an individual can do and because it more adequately addresses the seven basic clinical assessment issues (Muma, 1983, 1986, 1998). It is *practical* because it provides these teachers appropriate directions for activities in language intervention or teaching. Furthermore, it is *practical* because it fulfills the professional responsibility to provide appropriate educational services to each individual who is deaf or hard of hearing.

> *Such perspectives are both useful and practical.*

Constructionism

Searle (1992) showed that constructionism provides the most coherent account of language acquisition. Therefore, it is necessary to follow constructionism in grammatical assessment.

The basic tenet of constructionism is that an individual is an active processor of information; that is, an individual actively processes cognitive, social, emotional, and cultural aspects of his or her world toward establishing an experiential base for language acquisition. Such experiential bases have been regarded as knowledge of the world (Lakoff, 1987), possible worlds (Bruner, 1986), situated minds (Nelson, 1996), and the four levels of the cognitive social bases of language acquisition (Muma, 1998). The assessment implications of these issues are:

Constructionism provides an appropriate view for language assessment.

a. It is necessary to ascertain what an individual can do in actual social commerce simply because it is in that context that an individual is actively processing in daily life.

b. The prima facie evidence of active processing is spontaneous, as opposed to elicited, speech/signing.

c. It is necessary to base grammatical assessment on representative samples of speech/signing issuing from the twelve different kinds of contexts that underwrite language acquisition (Nelson, 1985).

d. The goals of grammatical assessment are to ascertain an individual's available repertoires, progress in acquisition sequences, strategies of learning, and active loci of learning.

Theoretical Perspectives

The five most influential theories of language acquisition over the previous four decades provide appropriate perspectives for assessment.

Within philosophical views, theoretical perspectives provide understandings and explanations (Kaplan, 1964). It is precisely because it is necessary to understand why grammatical assessment is carried out in particular ways that it is necessary to know which theoretical perspectives underwrite such assessments. Perera (1994), the editor of the *Journal of Child Language*, identified the five most influential theories of language acquisition over the previous twenty-five years. These theories have been relatively successful in meeting the necessary criteria for theoretical adequacy: descriptive adequacy, explanatory adequacy, and empirical adequacy. Relevance theory (Sperber & Wilson, 1986) as the newest rendition of speech acts theory (Grice, 1975), bootstrapping theories (Gleitman, 1994; Pinker, 1984), and learnability theories (Lightfoot, 1989; Pinker, 1984; Wexler, 1994) are especially useful in language assessment.

It is important to note that reinforcement theory was not cited by Perera simply because the literature has long since shown that reinforcement theory does not provide a viable account of language acquisition (Bruner, 1981; Cazden, 1988; Chomsky, 1968; Nelson, 1985; Pinker, 1988; Searle, 1992). Rather, intent has emerged as offering a more viable account of language acquisition. This means that language assessment should be based on representative samples of spontaneous (intentional) speech/signing in actual social commerce where cognitive, social, emotional, and cultural influences are at work.

> *Reinforcement is no longer regarded as a viable account of language acquisition.*

Also, the modality theory (Osgood, 1957) was not mentioned by Perera (1994). This theory had been replaced by speech acts (Grice, 1975) and relevance theories (Sperber & Wilson, 1986) because these theories provided a more viable account of information processing.

> *The modality view of language has been replaced by speech acts and relevance theories.*

Muma (1998) delineated fifteen major substantive issues in **cognition** that pertain to language acquisition. The Vygotskian perspective offers a viable appreciation of the **social bases** of language acquisition (Hagstrom, herein; Rogoff, 1990; Wertsch, 1991, 1998). An individual's **emotional** state plays a significant role in language acquisition (Brown, 1977; Bloom & Beckwith, 1988). Furthermore, an individual's parents, siblings, peers, and teachers all play significant roles both *socially* and *culturally* in language acquisition. Indeed, language acquisition is "a process of cognitive socialization" (Brown, 1956, p. 247). Accordingly, it is necessary to consider the core CCCE issues in assessment, indeed in intervention as well.

> *The CCCE perspective addresses the core issues of language.*

Three of the theories cited by Perera either hold that intent is the

| *Relevance theory, bootstrapping theory, and learnability theory have emerged as providing appropriate accounts of language acquisition.* |

central issue of language, or what Bruner (1981, 1986) regarded as the irreducible nucleus of language, or are compatible with this assumption; those theories were (1) relevance theory (Sperber & Wilson, 1986); (2) bootstrapping theory (Gleitman, 1994; Pinker, 1984), government and binding theory (Chomsky, 1982) and parameter setting theory (Lightfoot, 1989); which are the parents of (3) learnability theory (Pinker, 1984; Wexler, 1994). Transformational generative grammar (Chomsky, 1957, 1965) set the stage for what later became government and binding theory. These theories have the following implications for grammatical assessment:

a. The prima facie evidence of what an individual can do with language is what that individual does with language in actual social commerce as opposed to elicited performance on contrived tasks (Muma, 1986, 1998).
b. The core issues of language are cognition, codification, communication, and expression (affect) rather than the modality view (expressive/receptive modalities) (Clark & Clark, 1977).
c. Contexts are crucial (Bruner, 1981).
d. Evidence of grammatical repertoires should be obtained for the basic relations evidenced in varied subject-verb-object constructions (Bloom, 1973).
e. Predication is the focal issue of grammar (Gleitman, 1994).
f. Evidence of productivity (Ingram, 1989) or lexical variation (Bloom, Rispoli, Gartner, & Hafitz, 1989) is needed to draw conclusions about an individual's grammatical abilities.

It should be stressed that eclectic views are inappropriate simply because they undermine scholarship. That is, philosophical views provide coherent frameworks and theoretical perspectives provide disci-

| *Eclectic views undermine scholarship.* |

plined understandings. Eclectic views intrude on cohesion and disciplined understandings, thereby undermining scholarship. In contrast, when views and perspectives are compatible, it is appropriate to incorporate them into a unified perspective.

Seven Basic Clinical Assessment Issues

Muma (1983, 1986, 1998) delineated seven basic clinical assessment issues that provide a model for language assessment. Figure 9.1 shows these issues as they relate to descriptive evidence and psychometric test scores.

	Descriptive Evidence	Psychometric Test Scores
Complaint	Yes	Yes
Problem/no problem	Yes	(Yes)
Nature of problem	Yes	No
Individual differences	Yes	No
Intervention implications	Yes	No
Prognosis	?	?
Accountability/efficacy	Yes	(Yes)

Figure 9.1. Seven basic clinical assessment issues as they relate to descriptive evidence and psychometric testing.

The **complaint** is a concern that an individual may have difficulties of some sort. Both descriptive and psychometric approaches address this issue by virtue of identifying the individual who may have difficulties and a statement from the referring source about the presumed nature of the problem.

> *A clinical complaint is a concern for someone.*

The **problem/no problem** issue is addressed differently by these two approaches. Descriptive evidence cites instances in which the language of the individual differs from that of his or her peers. In a sense, there is a normative comparison with descriptive evidence but it is not a psychometric norm. This kind of norm is intuitive knowledge by a fluent speaker of a language, who judges that a particular aspect of verbal behavior does not fit the intended language. In contrast, psychometric test performance

> *Both descriptive assessments and psychometric tests address the problem/no problem issue.*

for an individual is compared to a test norm. The standard criterion for such comparisons is two standard deviations from the mean in a negative direction. That is, if a score is more than two standard deviations below the mean, that performance is deemed to be a problem.

Reliance on extreme scores for ascertaining a problem raises another issue; it is "assessment power." Scholars in test development are well aware of the assessment power problem: when extreme scores are obtained, a test loses assessment power. When that happens, it is inap-

Tests have a special problem because they lose power for extreme scores.

propriate to draw conclusions about the individual and the test because such performances are likely to be due to a set of unknown extraneous variables rather than what a test presumably assesses. Thus, the occurrence of extreme scores raises a paradox. On the one hand, such scores would indicate a problem; yet, on the other hand, it may be inappropriate to draw conclusions about an individual's abilities in the event that the test lost the power to assess what it claims to assess.

Another side of the problem/no problem issue has to do with performance within a normative range. This raises three major assessment issues: objectivity, construct validity, and necessary and sufficient evidence.

A time-honored notion about psychometric tests is that they provide **objective** evidence whereas descriptive evidence was thought to provide

The objectivity claim for tests is a myth.

subjective evidence. This kind of thinking is seriously flawed. Philosophers have addressed the objectivity issue for several decades. The bottom line is that all human endeavors, including tests and their norms, are

inherently subjective (Lakoff, 1987). In test development (going in) and in test use (going out) the whole enterprise is laden with subjectivity. In test development, various decisions are made about what the test will be like, such as the content, format, scoring, nature of the norms, and types of validity. These are all subjective issues. Whether an individual scores in the normative range or aberrantly, the scores still have to be interpreted which is a subjective endeavor. It is simply a myth that psychometric tests provide objective evidence.

All assessments should be construct-based.

The field of test and measurement has shown that all assessment must have **construct validity** as defined from a theoretical perspective (Messick,

1980). That is precisely why this chapter began with philosophical views and theoretical perspectives that underwrite language assessment. *"All measurement should be construct referenced"* (Messick, 1975, p. 957). *"All* validity is at its base some form of construct validity. . . .It *is* the basic meaning of validity" (Guion, 1977, p. 410).

Unfortunately, we have been unable to find language tests that have construct validity as defined from a theoretical perspective. Muma and Brannon (1986) reviewed the ten most widely used language tests in speech-language pathology and found that none had appropriate construct validity. Indeed, a similar review this year yielded the same results (Muma, forthcoming). Most tests claim to have construct validity but they merely present elaborate tables for trait analysis or factor analysis; they do not show how a particular test was derived from a theoretical perspective. This means that these tests are

> *Even though many language tests claim to have construct validity, they are not based on theories of language acquisition.*

nothing more than the test developer's biases sanctioned by norms. Thus, they miss or subvert the crucial issue of construct validity.

As for **necessary and sufficient evidence**, the psychometric tests come up short, embarrassingly short. The literature from the major language scholars indicate that it is necessary to ascertain an individual's repertoire (intentional, semantic, grammatical, phonological, pragmatic) (Ninio, Snow, Pan, & Rollins, 1994), progress in acquisition sequences (Brown, 1973), alternative learning strategies (Goldfield & Snow, 2001), and active loci of learning (Bloom, Hood, & Lightbown, 1974; Muma, 1986, 1998). "Describing speaker's repertoires of communicative intents and rules for expressing those intents is crucial to any complete description of the language capacity" (Ninio, Snow, Pan, & Rollins, 1994, p. 157).

> *The language tests do not provide necessary and sufficient evidence of what an individual can do with language in actual social commerce.*

Brown (1973) indicated that rate of learning is notoriously varied whereas sequence is highly stable. This means that professionals who claim expertise in language need to ascertain the progress that individuals have made in acquisition sequences rather than rely on rate of learning indices such as chronological age (CA), mental age (MA), language age (LA), grade level, and frequency or percentile rank.

Bloom (1973), Muma (1986), and Weir (1962) have identified active loci of learning. For example, Bloom, Hood, and Lightbown (1974)

Language tests do not provide evidence of active loci of learning.

showed that children typically do not spontaneously imitate things they know or do not know; rather, they spontaneously imitate those aspects of language that they are striving to learn. A child who is trying to learn possessiveness will not imitate *the hat* but he will imitate *my hat*. The bottom line is that psychometric tests do not provide necessary and sufficient evidence simply because they do not deal with repertoires, progress in acquisition sequences, available learning strategies, and active loci of learning.

Language tests do not provide evidence of an individual's repertoire, progress in acquisition sequences, strategies, or active loci of learning.

Returning to the seven basic clinical assessment issues, descriptive evidence addresses the **nature of a problem** but psychometric tests do not. Because descriptive procedures deal with repertoires, progress in acquisition sequences, available strategies of learning, and active loci of learning, they provide evidence concerning the nature of a problem. It is precisely because psychometric tests do not address these issues that they do not deal with the nature of a problem.

Descriptive evidence more fully addresses **individual differences** or heterogeneity than psychometric tests. Inasmuch as repertoires, progress in acquisition strategies, alternative learning strategies, and active loci of learning vary from individual to individual,

Language tests abrogate individual differences.

descriptive evidence addresses individual differences whereas psychometric tests essentially abrogate or ignore these differences and focus on the degree to which a performance compares to a norm.

Strangely, the field of speech-language pathology has imposed the

The normative assumption has been imposed on the definition of specific language impairment.

normative mentality on its efforts to define **specific language impairment** (Tager-Flusberg & Cooper, 1999). Leonard (1989) attempted to define specific language impairment in terms of low phonetic substance, following learnability theory (Pinker, 1984). His efforts were undone by the heterogeneous nature of this population.

Muma (1991) held that if *specific* is regarded as the product of descriptive evidence that specifies an individual's repertoires, progress in acquisition sequences, available learning strategies, and active loci of learning, then the heterogeneous nature of clinical populations would be more appropriately addressed. By doing so, *specific language impairment* would obtain a more appropriate meaning than the psychometric version. Until special education is willing to address heterogeneity, it will haunt special education to the core (Muma, 1986, 1998).

> Specific *should be regarded as the product of specifying an individual's repertoires, progress in acquisition sequences, strategies, and active loci of learning.*

In a word, **heterogeneity** is characteristic of all clinical populations. Baumeister (1984), one of the foremost scholars in the field of mental retardation, indicated that the most outstanding characteristic of mental retardation is heterogeneity. "The heterogeneity of deaf children is, perhaps, the most complex factor affecting how they learn best and consequently how they are taught" (Stewart & Kluwin, 2001, p. xi). Muma (1978, 1986, 1998) indicated that language impaired individuals are notoriously heterogeneous. Therefore, it is necessary to employ assessment and

> *Assessment approaches should address heterogeneity explicitly.*

intervention approaches that explicitly address heterogeneity rather than the traditional homogeneity-motivated approaches, such as CA, MA, LA, grade norms, and frequency counts.

Language assessments based on descriptive issues cited above more adequately deal with **intervention implications** or teaching than normative test scores. This is so because descriptive evidence dealing with available repertoires, progress in acquisition sequences, alternative learning strategies, and active loci of learning provide appropriate goals for language acquisition. More specifically, language intervention or teaching should focus on expanding repertoires, following acquisition sequences, utilizing available

> *Intervention implications are provided by descriptive assessment.*

learning strategies, and active loci of learning. Psychometric tests and checklists simply do not have these potentials.

As for **prognosis**, neither descriptive evidence nor psychometric test scores provide appropriate evidence. The literature simply does not have

> *Neither descriptive evidence nor psychometric test scores provide appropriate evidence for prognosis.*

the necessary evidence to provide accurate prognostic statements. The main problem for prognosis is that language acquisition typically occurs in spurts (Brown, 1973). We do not know when a spurt will occur, what will be learned during the spurt, nor how long a spurt will last. Needless to say, prognostic statements are merely intuitive speculations. However, intuition is itself risky. "But perhaps we should not trust our intuitions. . ." (Wanner, 1988, p. 82).

> *Evidence for accountability or efficacy is subtly complex and even deceptive.*

Accountability or efficacy is another basic assessment issue. The motivation to document accountability or efficacy is to account for the effects of intervention or teaching. Although it is desirable to substantiate the effects of intervention or teaching, this is a complex and potentially deceptive arena.

> *Simple pre-post comparisons of the data do not provide appropriate evidence of intervention effectiveness.*

First, it should be acknowledged that the documentation of change is one of the most difficult and complex issues facing research design. Simple pre-post comparisons yield questionable data because they could occur for a variety of reasons, some of which are independent of the particular kind of intervention. The mere act of giving special attention to a behavior could effectively change it. This is known as the Hawthorne Effect (Ventry & Schiavetti, 1986). It could be that any approach could be effective precisely because of Hawthorne Effects.

> *Appropriate evidence of intervention effectiveness include: expanded repertoires, progress in acquisition sequences, strategies, and active loci of learning.*

Any basic research design book (Schiavetti & Metz, 1997) conveys the message that mere pre-post comparisons constitute a "weak" design. It is necessary to have a Solomon Randomized Four-group design to adequately account for the effectiveness of an intervention or teaching approach. Yet, there are no studies that have used this design. This means that the best available evidence on accountability or efficacy is rationale evidence rather than empirical evidence. That is, the philosophical views and theoretical perspectives of professionals who render services constitute the most appropriate evidence of what should be done. In this regard, evidence of expanding repertoire, progress in acquisition sequences, utilization of alternative learning strategies, and exploitation of active loci of learning provide appropriate evidence.

The value of **rationale evidence** is underscored by the inherent heterogeneous nature of clinical populations. It is naive to pit one approach against another when dealing with heterogeneous populations. One approach may work well with one individual but not another. This does not mean that one approach is better than another.

> *Rational evidence is more appropriate than empirical evidence.*

The comparisons in Figure 9.1 between formal (psychometric normative tests, checklists, etc.) and informal (descriptive) approaches obviously favors the latter in addressing the seven basic clinical assessment issues. However, normative tests have useful applications, especially in assessing group performances, simply because of the underlying homogeneity assumption. Furthermore, it should be stressed that the U.S. Office of Education stated explicitly that "standardized assessment" could be achieved with the use of formal and/or informal measures and that academic achievement need not be considered in language assessment (Martin, 1980).

> *Informal approaches (descriptive measures) more fully address the seven basic clinical assessment issues than do formal measures (psychometric tests).*

Why Assess Grammatical Skills

Before addressing the need for a grammatical assessment, it is necessary to make a distinction between pregrammatical and grammatical individuals. Brown (1973) indicated that early word combinations may only be canonical combinations lacking grammatical status. Greenfield and Smith (1976) provided a developmental sequence for the emergence of semantic functions and relations preparatory to grammatical acquisition. Bloom (1973) indicated that the basic grammatical relations are varied subject-verb-object (SVO) relations. That position is in keeping with the verb as having the focal grammatical

> *It is necessary to make a distinction between pregrammatical and grammatical individuals.*

relations (Gleitman, 1994). Appendix C provides an outline of the analysis for dealing with these basic grammatical domains. These issues provide a useful way to distinguish between pregrammatical and grammatical individuals. A pregrammatical child is one who is not yet evidencing varied SVO constructions.

Assessment of the pregrammatical child is different from that of the grammatical child.

It is necessary to assess the following issues for pregrammatical children: seven early intentions (Halliday, 1975; Nelson, 1990), semantic functions and relations (Greenfield & Smith, 1976), experiential base (Bruner, 1986; Lakoff, 1987; Nelson, 1996), social-emotional base (Ainsworth, 1973; Rutter, 1979), and cognitive precursors (Bates & MacWhinney, 1979).

Assessment of the grammatical child should consider repertoires, progress in acquisition sequences, strategies, and active loci of learning.

As for grammatical individuals, it is necessary to assess the following: grammatical repertoires, progress in acquisition sequences, alternative learning strategies, active loci of learning, pragmatic parameters, and phonological skills. The focus of this chapter is grammatical repertoire, acquisition sequences, learning strategies, and active loci of learning. Several different sources have identified acquisition sequences, alternative strategies of learning, and active loci of learning (Bloom & Lahey, 1978; Muma, 1978, 1986, 1998).

Rather than frequencies, it is necessary to provide evidence of expanding repertoires.

Rather than frequencies (or percentages), it is necessary to ascertain an individual's grammatical competencies in terms of grammatical systems for SVO. Brown (1973) showed that the object nominal system (NP2) is learned first and more elaborately than the subject nominal system (NP1). Thus, it is necessary to ascertain grammatical repertoires for NP1 and NP2 separately.

Chomsky's (1965) theory of transformational generative grammar provides a useful way to appreciate the auxiliary system in SVO. Chomsky's (1982) subsequent government and binding theory expanded and elaborated on his previous theory by incorporating semantic constraints, syntactic constraints, phonological constraints, pragmatic constraints, and default conditions. Furthermore, Harris (1965) delineated the basic verbals of English. Thus, a grammatical assessment should strive to ascertain an individual's repertoire for the following grammatical systems: NP1, NP2, auxiliary, verbal, and grammatical operations or transformations. Appendix C outlines the basic kinds of structures for these grammatical systems. Many variations can be obtained by combining

> *Theories of generative grammar provide useful ways of appreciating an individual's repertoire.*

various aspects. For example, an individual could evidence an elaborated nominal system (either NP1 or NP2) by incorporating adjectives, relative clauses, and relative clause deletions. Appendix D is a contrived language sample that is analyzed according to these structures and variations of these structures. Appendix E is a list of basic vocabulary for general routines that are likely to appear in their early grammatical constructions.

Becoming Operational

With these views and perspectives, professionals in deaf education could carry out an appropriate assessment of grammatical skills. The traditional view was to establish a baseline of where the child was in acquiring language. This was operationalized by counting the frequencies of a list of previously selected grammatical structures or by a checklist of grammatical categories, usually "parts of speech" and/or sentence types. Another form of baselining has been the conversion of frequencies

> *The baseline notion does not address repertoire, sequences, strategies, or active loci.*

into percentages. These do not address the crucial issues of what a child can do with language in actual social commerce, specifically repertoires, progress in acquisition sequences, strategies, and active loci of learning.

Another traditional notion was that sentence lengths, typically expressed as mean lengths of utterance (MLU) or T-unit lengths were deemed valid indices of language acquisition. However, these notions have been shown to be invalid, especially when MLU exceeds 4.25 (Brown, 1973). The valid range of MLU as an index of language acquisition is 1.0 to 4.25; thereafter, MLU becomes a performance index whereby the MLU varies more as a function of communicative contexts

> *Length of utterance is no longer considered a valid index of language acquisition except for Brown's Stage II.*

than as a function of language acquisition (Brown, 1973). While length of utterance is relatively easy to calculate, professionals have a responsibility to provide more valid measurements.

Two major developments occur when MLU is about 4.25 that undermine MLU as a valid index of language acquisition. They are optional deletions and pronominalization. The following illustrate how sentences can become shorter, yet grammatically more complex, by incorporating optional deletions and pronominalization.

> *When a child can optionally delete and pronominalize, some short utterances are grammatically more complex than some longer utterances.*

MLU

10   The big brown horse will win some races.
9   The big brown horse will win some.
7   The big brown horse will win.
6   The big brown horse will.
5   The big horse will.
4   The horse will
3   It will.

Three other problems with MLU are poor reliability (Klee & Fitzgerald, 1985), excessive variance (Lahey, 1994), and how the Miller and Chapman (1981) norms were calculated (Conant, 1987). As for reliability, once MLU exceeds 4.25, language samples from one child may vary greatly within a single day or two. This certifies the view that MLU is no longer an acquisition index but is a performance index. The issue of excessive variance also undermines the MLU value simply because the variances overlap across age-levels and across Brown's five stages, thereby undermining the MLU as a legitimate index. Unfortunately for the Miller and Chapman (1981) MLU norms, Conant (1987) discovered a serious calculation error; it was that these norms stripped away the variance by utilizing the midpoints of the reported samples. The result was MLU norms that were deceptively "clean." When the full range of the data are incorporated, the problem of excessive variance emerges.

> *The MLU has poor reliability, excessive variances, and a very short range as an index of language acquisition.*

It is generally true that there is a positive relationship between sentence length and emerging complexity, especially within the MLU range of 1.00 to 4.25 morphemes (Brown, 1973), and even beyond.

However, Brown cautioned that length of utterance beyond 4.25 morphemes is hopelessly confounded with performance variable rather than acquisition variables, thereby making repertoires for grammatical systems and progress in acquisition sequences "cleaner" perspectives for ascertaining language acquisition than length of utterances. "By the time the child reaches Stage V, however, he is able to make constructions of such great variety that what he happens to say and the MLU of a sample begin to depend more on the character of the interaction than on what the child knows, and so the index loses its value as an indicator of grammatical knowledge" (p. 54).

> *MLU is hopelessly confounded with performance when a child reaches an MLU of 4.25.*

The T-unit (Hunt, 1964) has been offered as an option to the mean length of utterance (MLU). Even though it has received wide attention more recently (White, Scott, & Grant, 2002), it also is subject to performance variation.

The current scholarly literature has put these notions aside because they lack appropriate justifications. Rather than frequencies and length of utterances, it is necessary to deal with contexts. Nelson (1985) delineated twelve different kinds of contexts that pertain to language acquisition. The most relevant contexts for assessing grammatical skills are intention or agenda context, situational context, and linguistic context. Under the assumption of the intentional context, Gleitman (1994) showed that what is said (linguistic context) provides linguistically sanctioned information about the nature of language. Furthermore, she indicated

> *Nelson (1985) delineated twelve different contextual influences in language acquisition.*

that what is perceived about an ongoing event or topic provides cognitive information that supports the meaning of what is said. This means that it is inappropriate to have a previously selected list of grammatical categories for grammatical assessment or rely on length of utterances. Rather, it is necessary to ascertain an individual's available repertoire (Ninio et al., 1994), progress in acquisition sequences (Bloom & Lahey, 1978; Muma, 1978, 1986, 1998), alternative strategies of learning (Muma, 1978, 1986, 1998), and active loci of learning (Bloom, Hood, & Lightbown, 1974; Muma, 1978, 1986, 1998). Thus, diagnostic teaching should shift to these issues.

By dealing with grammatical repertoire, progress in acquisition sequences, strategies of learning, and active loci of learning, teachers of the deaf are provided with appropriate information for establishing language intervention targets or goals. One goal is to expand an individual's repertoire for those aspects of grammar that evidence relatively meager skills. Teachers should decide which grammatical system(s) should be expanded.

> *Expanding grammatical repertoires should be goals for intervention.*

A second goal is to assist a child through various acquisition sequences. For example, if a child uses tag-questions, the goal would be to proceed by using inflected questions, true yes/no questions, and then various *wh*-questions. A third goal would be to utilize the acquisition strategies employed by a child.

> *Another goal is to assist children through acquisition sequences.*

For example, if the child is a message learner, as opposed to a code learner, the child's strategy should be incorporated in teaching. The forth goal is to focus on those aspects of language in which a child evidences active loci of learning. For example, if a child has "build-ups" that reveal new loci such as tense changing, those loci should be the goals of teaching or intervention.

> *Two other goals are to exploit the strategies of learning that the children are using and focus on the children's active loci of learning.*

Even though this chapter deals with grammatical assessment, perhaps two pragmatic issues that are evidenced in grammar should be incorporated. They are deictic reference and anaphora; both are problematic with the hard of hearing.

> *Professionals should address deictic reference.*

Deictic reference is the use of grammatical structure to distinguish between the speaker and listener perspectives. Possessiveness and demonstratives have this function. For example, the following sentences make distinctions between the speaker and listener.

My hat is blue.

Your hat is red.

That pencil is blue.

This pencil is red.

Anaphora is the use of pronominal forms to maintain the reference for previously identified referents (Lust, 1986a, b). There are three issues related to anaphoric reference: loading, competition, and vacant anaphora (Muma, 1986, 1998). Anaphoric loading occurs when anaphora extends over more that one instance. For example, anaphoric loading occurred in three instances in the following example.

Professionals should address anaphora.

Billy went downtown.

<u>He</u> rode his bike.

<u>He</u> rode through a mud puddle.

<u>He</u> got wet.

Anaphoric competition occurs when two or more anaphoric references occur. In a sense, they compete for mental processing space while other processing occurs for sentence comprehension. The following example evidences competing anaphora for the reference to *Sue* and to the *ice cream cone*.

Sue bought an ice cream cone.

<u>She</u> took <u>it</u> to the store.

<u>She</u> dropped <u>it</u>.

<u>It</u> made a mess.

Vacant anaphora occurs when a person uses pronominal forms but does not identify their referents. The following is an example.

<u>They</u> went to the movie.

Then, <u>they</u> rode <u>their</u> car around town.

Conceptual Framework Revisited: Carrying Out the Assessment

Teachers of the deaf who have been trained appropriately to assess grammatical repertoire, progress in acquisition sequences, alternative strategies of learning, and active loci of learning are in a position to greatly advance their educational services to the deaf and hard of hearing simply because they are meeting the criteria for appropriate evidence, more specifically, relevance to the scholarly literature and relevance to an individual's repertoire. Such evidence issues from representative samples of spontaneous speech/signing in actual social commerce.

Gallagher (1983) described three different kinds of representative language samples: complete, optimal, and typical. Complete and optimal language samples are virtually impossible to obtain because it would be necessary to follow an individual for months, even years, to sample all,

Language samples should be representative of what an individual can do.

or the best, that that individual can do with language. Therefore, it is necessary to obtain an individual's typical language sample (spoken/signed) from actual social commerce. In so doing, it is necessary to acknowledge the degree of sampling error that may accompany a typical sample.

Sampling error rate raises two other major issues: sample size and varied contexts. The prevailing language sample sizes in speech-language pathology have been 50 or 100 utterances (Muma, 1998). However, Brown (1973) indicated that it is necessary to have at least 200 utterances to draw conclusions about an individual grammatical repertoire. Thus, the question arises as to what the sampling error rates may be for 50-,

The prevailing language sample sizes have excessive error rates.

100-, and 200-utterance samples when compared to much larger samples, specifically 400-utterance samples. Muma et al. (1998) showed that the sampling error rates for 50-, 100-, and 200-utterance samples by three- and four-year-old children are about 55%, 40%, and 15%, respectively. It can safely be assumed that these error rates are greater for older children and adults because they are more likely to have larger grammatical repertoires. This means that published studies and clinical reports based on 50- or 100-utterance samples have excessive error rates. Efforts to ascertain grammatical repertoires should be based on at least 200 utterances in actual social commerce (Brown, 1973).

Context is crucial. "Context is all" (Bruner, 1981, p. 172). Nelson (1985) delineated twelve different kinds of contexts that influence language acquisition. Thus, it is a given that contextual

Where is the research that shows that elicited language and spontaneous language are comparable?

variations are likely to yield different verbal/signing performances. One shortcut that has been used is to rely on elicited language samples rather than spontaneous language samples. However, where is the research that shows that an individual's verbal (speech/signed) repertoire is comparable between elicited and spontaneous verbal behavior?

Inasmuch as spontaneous verbal behavior provides the prima facie evidence of what an individual can do with language because it is intentional, it behooves professionals in deaf education to rely on such evidence. Said differently, assumptions and conclusions about what an individual can do with language should be based on what that individual does in representative samples from actual social commerce. This rationale is in keeping with the central principle of speech acts theory (Grice, 1975; Searle, 1969), relevance theory (Sperber & Wilson, 1986), and bootstrapping theory (Gleitman, 1994; Pinker, 1984). The central principle of these theories is that messages are constructed to make intentions recognizable. Elicited samples are not intentional. The basic principle for bootstrapping theory is that messages that are used in actual social commerce are linguistically sanctioned and appropriate to the event and/or topic. Elicited samples do not have these characteristics.

> *Spontaneous language samples provide prima facie evidence of what an individual can do.*

Attribution Criteria

A crucial question emerges when faced with evidence concerning an individual's presumed grammatical skills. It is: What criteria should be used to attribute grammatical skills to an individual?

This issue should be considered from two perspectives, traditional practices and contemporary views from the scholarly literature. Traditionally, frequency counts were made; furthermore, these counts were usually converted to percentages with the ensuing claims that as an individual reaches 80%, 90%, or 100% correct performance, learning has occurred. This reflects the tired old habit strength principle. Unfortunately, such practices miss the crucial issue for documenting learning. It is that learning is evidenced when new things are acquired.

> *Frequency counts do not provide appropriate evidence of what an individual can do with language.*

Learnability theory (Lightfoot, 1989; Pinker, 1984) has shown that frequency is not a good index of grammatical learning. Somehow the field of speech-language pathology has missed this literature and has continued undaunted to rely on frequency counts and percentages. Cazden (1988) was dismayed that such views continue to be held: "To put the conclusions bluntly: Reinforcement did not exist, frequency did not correlate, and expansions did not help" (p. 281).

> *Learnability theory has shown that frequency is not a good way to establish learning.*

Attribution criteria should be based on contextual evidence.

The contemporary views over the past two decades hold that context is crucial as evidence of language acquisition. Therefore, attribution criteria should incorporate contextual evidence. This can be achieved in different ways: Piagetian attribution criteria, productivity, and robustness.

The Piagetian criteria are preparation, attainment, and consolidation. A behavior is deemed to be in **preparation** when it occurs infrequently, it is context-bound, and it is difficult to elicit (Muma, 1998).

Attribution could address preparation, attainment, and consolidation.

Thus, when an infant first says, "Mama," the infant would be in preparation for learning "Mama." A behavior is deemed to be **attained** when it is frequent, not context-bound, and easy to elicit. For example, when an infant says "Mama" frequently, in varied contexts, and it is easy to elicit, the infant is said to have attained the word *Mama*. Notice that frequency is tied to context and elicitation. A behavior is deemed to be **consolidated** when an individual can combine a particular grammatical aspect with another aspect. For example, consolidation is evidenced when a child can combine "Mama" with other aspects to form "Mama come," "Mama here," "my Mama."

Lexical variation is a way to establish grammatical productivity.

Productivity (Ingram, 1989; Lahey, 1988) is evidenced when a child has lexical variation for a particular structure (Bloom, Rispoli, Gartner, and Hafitz, 1989). Thus, if a child evidenced possessiveness with lexical variation, that child is deemed to have productive knowledge of that aspect of language. This is illustrated by the following:

my hat, my shoes, my Daddy

At least three structural variations in spontaneous speech are needed to attribute productivity (Bloom et al., 1989; Muma, 1998).

Robustness is another way to consider attribution.

Goldin-Meadow and Mylander (1984) studied gestural and grammatical communication in deaf children. They described grammatical skills that were "hearty" and "fragile." These two issues are dimensions of robustness (Muma, 1986, 1998). A hearty structure is one that is not responsive to modeling. For example, one child said, "Him go." When the two models "He go" and "He goes" were given, this child said, "Yah, him go." In contrast, subsequently, this child became responsive to modeling for this aspect of grammar. Then, when he would say, "Him here," he responded to the models "he here" or "he is here" by saying "He here." When he became responsive to modeling for a particular aspect of grammar, that aspect was deemed to be fragile.

Teacher as the Focal Professional

Needless to say, each individual with a hearing loss is the focus of all educational services. Furthermore, parents play focal roles as well.

The deaf education teacher is the focal person for rendering appropriate educational services. This person has the expertise, access to the school curriculum, access to the deaf or hard of hearing individuals, and access to their parents. Indeed, the parents are also focal participants in the educational services for their children. Thus, when language assessment is well done, intervention is half begun simply because the focal person is doing the assessment and has the best opportunities to implement the appropriate intervention issues, i.e., expand repertoire, follow acquisition sequences, exploit available learning strategies, and exploit active loci of learning. In doing so, the deaf education teacher would also incorporate the student's parents. Thus, educational services for individuals become a cooperate relationship between these individuals, their parents, and their deaf education teacher.

> *Students, parents, and professionals are all focal individuals for rendering appropriate services.*

138

Appendix A:

The Cognitive Socialization Approach, Views, and Perspectives of Language Acquisition

Approach

Cognitive socialization: The approach pertaining to language acquisition whereby the cognitive and social functions of language are emphasized, especially the centrality of communicative intent, and the structural aspects of language are subsumed.

Philosophical Views

Behaviorism: The view that behavior can be explained in terms of observable relationships between instances of behavior and reinforcement. A major problem for this view is that some crucial aspects of behavior, namely language and cognition, are based on internal mental states and processes, notably intent and inferencing. A popular undisciplined version of behaviorism is that almost anything, including internal mental states, is within the realm of reinforcement. Such views are too powerful to the extent that they explain nothing.

Constructionism: The view that individuals actively construct their knowledge of the world according to their experiences of living in the world. Such knowledge culminates in that person's possible worlds and situated mind.

Functionalism: The view that functions have priority over structure; structures are in the service of functions. In language, the primary cognitive functions are representation and mediation, whereas the primary communicative functions are intent and both explicit and implicit content. Furthermore, intent is the irreducible nucleus of language. This means that language structure is consciously constructed to make intent recognizable.

Innatism: The view that human beings are innately "wired" to function in particular ways. This view holds that humans are endowed with an innate capacity for language and that this capacity is unlike that of any other species. The language acquisition process proceeds in prescribed sequences, with varying rates, in accordance with the physiological maturation of the individual. This means that the manner and sequences of language acquisition are directed and constrained by the inherent nature of the cognitive system.

Monism/Dualism: The views that pertain to the mind/brain distinctions. If a view is only about the mind independent of the brain or the brain independent of the mind, it is a monistic view. Dualism takes into consideration the relationships between the mind and brain accounts. The extent to which either monism or dualism is structural rather than functional is the extent to which these views lack coherence. Materialism is a subcategory of monism pertaining to the brain. Materialism has the goal of accounting for neural architecture, physiology, and functions as the ultimate accounts of how the brain functions.

Quantification: The view that behavior can be converted to numbers for the purpose of better understandings. The philosophy literature has much to say about the hazards of converting behavior to numbers.

Reductionism: The view that complex behavior can be reduced to increasingly smaller units for better understandings and that these small units can be "reconstructed" toward a better understanding of complex behaviors. In language, the traditional notions of expressive and receptive language, visual/auditory processing, parts of speech, sentence types, and phonemes as the basic unit of speech production are reductionistic notions that have not held up in the contemporary literature.

Theoretical Perspectives

Bootstrapping theory: The perspective that one aspect of language acquisition provides a context for learning another aspect. For example, a child who does well with phonology could use this skill to assist in learning semantics, syntax, or pragmatics. Another child who does relatively well with syntax could use that skill to assist in learning phonology, semantics, and pragmatics.

Learnability theory: The innatist perspective that language acquisition is the result of unique and innate human faculties. Accordingly, language acquisition is governed largely by maturational processes. Rather than many instances, an individual can learn from one, or a few, instances whereby the individual's available repertoire is ready to assimilate the new instances. Indeed, an individual can expand one's knowledge not only with contact with a language, but also by derivation.

Modality theory: The perspective that the modalities of language such as expression (speaking, writing, signing) and reception (listening, reading, understanding sign) are uniquely different and constitute the essence of language. Unfortunately, this view pervades much of education, notably special education. It is unfortunate because this view overlooks the core cognition, codification, communication, and expression (affect) (CCCE) aspects of language.

Modularity theory: The perspective that the brain is organized in such a manner that particular regions function autonomously, notably the primary sensory and motor areas are to have encapsulated functions. In contrast, the secondary and tertiary areas that surround the primary sensory and motor areas have rich and varied connections throughout their cortex, across to the opposite hemisphere, and to the limbic system. This means that modularity may be limited to the primary sensory and motor areas; and it means that language operates on general cognition rather than a unique faculty.

Reinforcement theory: The perspective that reinforcement can govern, direct, and control behavior. This view has been extended to claims to deal with learning but the literature has raised serious questions about the legitimacy of such claims, especially in the failure to "transfer," or generalize, failure to adequately account for internal mental states such as intent.

Relevance theory: The perspective that cognition comprises a crucial substantive base of language and that socialization comprises another crucial substantive base of language. Furthermore, it holds that the irreducible nucleus of language is intent and that the function of structure is to make intent recognizable.

Speech acts theory: This theory expanded the study of language to focus on intent as the irreducible nucleus of language, the linguistic nature of a message, the two-dimensional nature of content (explicit content: basic ideas entailed in a message; implicit content: knowledge of the world or possible worlds that makes explicit content meaningful), and the effects of a message on a listener.

Appendix B:

Forty Issues That Deaf Education Should Address

Forty issues that special education, speech-language pathology, and deaf education should address to become aligned with major substantive developments in the scholarly cognitive socialization literature.

1. Cognitive socialization as the most encompassing perspective.
2. Cognitive social bases of language: A model.
3. Who do we think we are? Which philosophical views underwrite the educational services.
4. The five most influential theories of language acquisition.
5. The language modality fallacy.
6. Core issues of language: Cognition, codification, communication, and expression.
7. Centrality of intent.
8. Informativeness: Propositioning propositions.
9. Speech acts and relevance: Four main issues.
10. Specific language impairment (SLI): *Specific* as the product of specifying.
11. Cognition: Possible worlds, situated minds.
12. Cognition: Brute and institutional facts, natural categories.
13. Memory-as-entity fallacy replaced by memory specific to a task.
14. Piagetian issues: Insufficiently human.
15. Codification: Message-of-best-fit to make intent recognizable.
16. Semantic assessment: Three basic issues.
17. Brown's five stages and MLU: Lack validity.
18. Language sampling: Error rates for sample size.
19. Grammatical assessment: Repertoire, sequences, strategies, and active loci of learning.
20. Attribution criteria.
21. Language tests: Lack construct validity.
22. Heterogeneity: Haunts the clinical fields to the core.

23. Normative tests: Thirteen questionable issues.
24. Language assessment: Seven basic issues.
25. Official standardized assessment: Formal and/or informal.
26. Communication: Transition from expression to language.
27. Pragmatics: From language to message, including deictic and anaphoric references.
28. Multiculturalism: Diversity.
29. Pregrammatical child.
30. Grammatical child.
31. Parent participation: Three levels.
32. Peer modeling.
33. Intervention: The parallel talk strategy.
34. Intervention: Teaching or facilitation.
35. Intervention: Expanding experiential worlds.
36. Intervention: Expanding social-emotional worlds.
37. The efficacy fallacy.
38. Technician or clinician.
39. Expediency fallacy: The bane of the clinical fields.
40. Facing change: Challenge or resistance.

Note: From "Challenge for Higher Education: Teaching the Cognitive Social Bases of Language," by S. Cloud and J. Muma, 1999, Issues in Higher Education, 3. Adapted with permission.

Appendix C:

Basic Grammatical Structures

The basic kinds of structures for subject nominal (MP1), object nominal (NP2), auxiliary, and verbal systems and grammatical operations.

Nominal Systems (NP1 & NP2):
    Proper noun: Mama, Billy, Mrs. Jones,...
    Definite pronoun: I, he, she, they,...
    Indefinite pronoun: some, one, everyone, nobody, anything, somebody, no one, everything,...
    Determiner + noun:
    Determiner:
    Definite article: the
    Indefinite article: a, some, (null)
    Possessive: my, your, their,...
    Demonstrative: this, that, these, those
    Number:
        cardinal: 1, 2, 9, 27,...
        ordinal: first, second, ninth,...
    Noun: animate, inanimate
    Derived nominals:
    ToV: to work, to run, to smile,...
    Ving: working, running, smiling,...
    For/to: for him to work, for them to run,...
    That + sentence: that he worked,...

Auxiliary System: C + (modal) + (aspect)
    C (concordance):
    C1: present tense
    C2: past tense
    Modal:
        C1: can, will, shall, may, must
        C2: could, would, should, might, must
    Aspect: (have + participle) + (be + ing)

Verbal System:

BE + adjective	I am happy.
BE + noun phrase(NP)	I am a friend.
BE + adverb-place	I am here.
Intransitive	I fell.
Transitive + NP	I ate a cookie.
Vh + NP	I have a friend.
Vs + adjective	I seem happy.
Vb + adjective/NP	I became happy/a friend.

Operations/transformations:

Yes/No question
Do
Wh- question
NOT
Adjective
Relative clause
Relative clause deletion
Particle shift
Conjoin
Emphatic
Contraction
Noun deletion
Noun phrase deletion
Ellipsis
There/here
Intensifier
Quote
Demonstration

Auxiliary Expansion:

C1: He works.
C2: He worked.
C1 modal(M): He can work.
C2 modal(M): He could work.
C1 have + participle: He has worked.
C2 have + participle: He had worked.

C1 be + ing: He is working.

C2 be + ing: He was working.

C1 have + part. + be + ing: He has been working.

C2 have + part. + be + ing: He had been working.

C1 M + have + part.: He shall have worked.

C2 M + have + part.: He should have worked.

C1 M + be + ing: He will be working.

C2 M + be + ing: He would be working.

C1 M + have + part. + be + ing: (ungrammatical)

C2 M + have + part. + be + ing:

　　He could have been working.

Appendix D:

Analyzed Language Sample

A contrived language sample that is analyzed according to
its basic grammatical systems and operations.

1. **Tom opened the box.**
   Proper N C2 VT Definite art. Ni
2. **He had found a baseball glove.**
   Def. pronoun C2 Have + Participle VT Indef. art. <u>Adjective</u> Ni
3. **No one found the price tag.**
   Indef. pronoun C2 Definite art. <u>Adjective</u> Ni
4. **It did not cost three dollars.**
   Definite pronoun C2 <u>Do</u> <u>Not</u> Vh #ordinal Ni
5. **Tom should put the glove that was in the box under the tree.**
   Proper N C2 Modal VT Definite art. Ni <u>Relative Cl.</u>
   <u>Relative Cl. Del.</u>
6. **His dog is a puppy.**
   Poss. Na C1 BE Indefinite art. Na
7. **It is pretty.**
   Definite pronoun C1 BE Adjective
8. **It is under the tree.**
   Definite pronoun C1 BE Adverb-place
9. **It is smelling the glove.**
   Definite pronoun C2 be + ing VT Definite art. Ni

<u>NP1 System:</u>
   Proper Noun: Tom
   Definite Pronoun: it
   Indefinite Pronoun: someone
   Poss. Na: his dog

<u>NP2 System:</u>
   Definite art. Ni: the box, the glove
   Definite art. Adjective Ni: the price tag

Definite art. Ni Relative Cl. Relative Cl. Del.:
    the glove that was in the box under the tree
Indefinite art. Na: a puppy
#ordinal Ni: three dollars
Indefinite art. Adjective Ni: a baseball glove

Auxiliary System:

C1: is
C2: opened
C2 Modal: should
C2 have + participle: had found
C2 be + ing: was smelling

Verbal System:

BE + NP: is a puppy
BE + Adjective: is pretty
BE + Adverb-place: is under the tree
VT: open the box, found a baseball glove
Vh + NP: cost

Grammatical Operations:

Do: did
Not: Not
Adjective + Noun: baseball glove
Rel. Clause + Rel. Clause Del.: <u>that was in the box</u>
                                    <u>under the tree</u>

Some adverbials:

Where	He is <u>in the house</u>.
When	He ate <u>last night</u>.
How	He worked <u>hard</u>.
Why	He worked <u>so they could play</u>.

Appendix E:
Basic Vocabulary for General Routines

Bathroom
  Nouns: toilet, tub, sink, soap, shampoo, toothbrush, toothpaste, mirror, hair brush, comb, deodorant, washcloth, towel, shower, bath, water
  Verbs: wash, brush, scrub, dry, clean, comb, fill

Bedroom
  Nouns: bed, sheet, blanket, pillow, dresser, closet, hanger, shirt, pants, underwear, shoes, tennis shoes, socks, pajamas, mirror, chair, rug, lights
  Verbs: sleep, rest, dress, change clothes, hang up, put away, clean up

Living room
  Nouns: chair, sofa, TV, CDs, CD player, rug, carpet, newspaper, magazine, lights
  Verbs: sit, stand, walk, lay down, vacuum, clean, dust, read, watch TV

Kitchen
  Nouns: table, chair, spoon, knife, fork, plate, cup, bowl, glass, cupboard, refrigerator, oven, stove, pot, pan, trash
  Verbs: make, cook, fry, bake, boil, clean up, sweep, pour, cut, open, close, pick up, set the table

Yard
  Nouns: axe, saw, shovel, ladder, hammer, nails, screws, screwdriver, cart, wheelbarrow, paint, brush, hose, sprinkler, grass, weeds
  Verbs: rake, walk, run, fall, watch, look, hoe, rake, shovel, dig, wash, spray, cut, mow

Glossary

Accountability: A basic assessment issue; the act of providing evidence that presumably documents the effectiveness of intervention.

Acquisition sequences: The orders, or sequences, for acquiring various skills. For example, tag-questions and inflected questions precede fully developed yes/no questions.

Active loci of learning: Those aspects of language acquisition in which a child is striving to learn at any given moment. Evidence of such active loci is typically found in language samples from actual social commerce.

Actual social commerce: Spontaneous social interaction in the real world.

Anaphora: The function of pronominal forms to maintain the identity of reference; three ways of observing anaphora: vacant anaphora, anaphoric loading, and competing anaphora.

A posteriori views or approaches: Those assessment or intervention approaches that are addressed as functions of what an individual does in actual social commerce.

Appropriation: The process of taking something (a behavior) that belongs to others and making it one's own.

A priori views or approaches: Those assessment or intervention approaches that are set before seeing a child; such approaches often subjugate the child by making the child conform to the previously established tasks.

Assessment power: The realm of assessment in which legitimate conclusions can be made about an individual's abilities, the normative range of 1.5 standard deviations below and above the mean.

Authoritarianism: Authoritarian edicts proclaiming the value of issues or points of view.

Behaviorism: The view that behavior can be explained in terms of observable relationships between instances of behavior and reinforcement.

Bootstrapping theory: Several language acquisition theories that indicate that some critical degree of accomplishment in one aspect of language will facilitate learning other aspects. For example, a child who has relatively good phonology could use that accomplishment to learn about syntax.

Capricious: Fanciful, whimsical, arbitrary.

Catalyst Grant: A federal grant to deaf education to avail itself of developing technologies.

CCCE perspective: The core of language: cognition, codification, communication, and expression.

Codification: Linguistic and nonlinguistic ways of coding messages.

Cognition: One's cognitive or mental abilities.

Cognitive socialization: The view that language acquisition is based on cognitive and social functions of language and that structure is subsumed.

Coherent: Rational, logically meaningful.

Collaborative learning: Learning occurs in a social nexus; it occurs with others.

Communication: The act of making intent recognizable.

Complaint (assessment): A basic assessment issue; a statement of concern that identifies an individual and the presumed nature of a problem.

Constructionism: The view that learners are active processors of information; issues of content, sequence, pacing, and intent are the province of the learner.

Construct validity: The theoretical and empirical justification for a particular assessment.

Content (explicit): The basic ideas entailed in a message.

Content (implicit): Knowledge of the world, possible worlds, or situated minds that make explicit content meaningful.

Data or evidence: Data is any kind of index, but evidence is data that meets the twofold criteria of being relevant to an individual's available repertoire and relevant to the contemporary scholarly literature.

Deaf culture: The ecology in which individuals who are deaf function.

Deictic reference: The linguistic mechanisms that separate the speaker and listener perspectives, i.e., mine/yours, here/there, this/that.

Descriptive adequacy: Evidence that a theory meets the following criteria: formal, simple, complete, and noncontradictory.

Dialogicality: Things that are deemed by social, cultural, and emotional influences worth learning maintain their inherent cultural voices even when individuals have unique applications for them.

Discrepancy learning: A cognitive theory that shows that variation is crucial for learning; it dethrones the traditional notions of drill and repetition.

Dogma: Unsubstantiated opinion.

Ecological validity: Behaviors that are observed in a child's real world, rather than on contrived tasks, are ecologically valid.

Embodiment: An infant's bodily experiences in the course of daily living that lead to schema development.

Emotional base: An individual's previous emotional or affective experiences that contribute to that person's possible worlds or situated mind.

Empirical adequacy: Providing data to support or refute an issue or theory.

Empirical brutism: Relying only on data; lacking rational evidence.

Empiricism: Providing data to support an issue.

Experiential base: An individual's previous experiences that result in that person's possible worlds or situated mind.

Explanatory adequacy: Providing evidence pertaining to mental processing or developmental evidence to support or refute an issue or theory.

Expression (affect): The affective or emotional aspect.

Force of authority: Exceeding to the expectations of institutions such as school demands.

Functionalism: The philosophical view that functions have priority over structure.

Heterogeneity: Individual differences.

Holy Trinity of psychometric salvation: The traditional belief that there are three options for valid assessment: content validity, criterion validity, and construct validity. This view has been dethroned, whereby construct validity is the essence of assessment and all other issues are derived from construct validity.

Homogeneity: Individuals who evidence the same characteristics.

Individual differences: A basic assessment issue: the differences in abilities and performances between one individual and another.

Intent: The irreducible nucleus of cognition and language.

Intervention implications: A basic assessment issue: The implicit information in assessment that directs intervention.

Irreducible nucleus of language: Intent is the essence of language; all issues concerning language should be derived from intent.

Language functions: The cognitive functions of language are representation and mediation; the communicative functions of language are intent and explicit content and implicit content.

Language structure: Intonations, speech sounds, words, phrases, clauses, sentences, paragraphs, stories, narratives, and discourse that serve to make intentions recognizable. Structures are in the service of language functions, especially intent.

Language transfers thinking: The act of codification is the act of conveying thought in ways to make intent recognizable; such acts can alter thought also.

Learnability theory: Innatists' proposals on the formal nature of language that are uniquely human in organization.

Mastery: The shift from initial and rather inept command of a skill to advanced and possibly superior skill.

Mimesis: Selective reenactment toward obtaining a skill.

Mindful learning: The continuous creation of new concepts or categories; openness to new information; an implicit awareness of the perceptions of others.

Modality perspective: The view that language operates in regard to the expressive (speaking, writing, signing) and receptive (listening, reading, comprehending sign) modalities.

National Agenda: A grass-roots effort to upgrade services for individuals who are deaf or hard of hearing.

Nature of a problem: A basic assessment issue: an individual's available repertoire, progress in acquisition sequences, strategies of learning, and active loci of learning that *specify* the nature of a problem.

Necessary and sufficient evidence: Evidence that is necessary and sufficient to draw conclusions about an individual's presumed skills.

Objectivity: Neutral or "God's-eye view"; free from human bias.

Ontological development: The acquisition of skills that are initially intermental (social and cultural) but subsequently become intramental (individualized within possible worlds).

Paternalism: The view that deaf or hard of hearing individuals should be protected because they are vulnerable to exploitation; they are presumably unable to do for themselves; this view leads to a state of dependency and helplessness.

Philosophical views: Those recognized views, positions, orientations, or models that provide coherent understandings and that underwrite theoretical perspectives.

Prima facie evidence: The best evidence, true evidence.

Problem/no problem: A basic assessment issue: Does a problem exist?

Prognosis: A basic assessment issue: the kinds of gains that are to be expected in a given period of time. Unfortunately, because of spurts of learning, the literature has been unable to provide valid prognostic evidence.

Rational evidence: The philosophical views and theoretical perspectives that comprise a logic for rendering educational services in particular ways.

Reductionism: Reducing language or other domains to small elements, and then building toward the whole.

Reinforcement: The presumed causal relationship between stimulus and response.

Relevance theory: The updated version of speech acts theory that broadened the study of language to deal with the centrality of intent, linguistic and nonlinguistic nature of messages, the relationships between implicit and explicit content, and the effects of a message on a listener.

Repertoire: The range of skills available to an individual.

Representative samples: Samples of behavior that characterize an individual's available skills; three kinds of representative samples: complete, optimal, and typical.

Schema: Preconceptual awareness.

Script: Social-emotional, and culturally determined roles for an individual's daily routines.

Semantic functions and relations: Basic ideas entailed in early one-, two-, and three-word utterances preparatory for grammatical skills.

Sideways learning: Appreciating alternative perceptions, explanations, and accounts of issues.

Simultaneity: Concepts, words, and actions are simultaneously an individual's and the social and cultural dynamics in which the individual functions.

Social base: An individual's previous social activities that contribute to that person's possible worlds or situated mind.

Socialization: The act of incorporating social, especially peer, influences on learning and behavior.

Speech acts theory: The language acquisition theory that established the centrality of intent and the cognitive social bases of learning.

Subjectivity: Affected by personal bias and emotional state.

Technology: The applied sciences, especially computer science.

Theoretical perspectives: Those perspectives that have become formalized into a theory and aspire to meet descriptive adequacy, explanatory adequacy, and empirical adequacy toward providing viable understandings, explanations, and predictions of what the theory posits.

Zone of proximal development: The degree of accomplishment that is evidenced when an individual benefits from the assistance of others.

References

Amabile, T., & Gitomer, J. (1984). Children's artistic creativity: Effects of choice in task materials. Personality and Social Psychology Bulletin 10, 209-215.

Anderson, J. (1983). The architecture of cognition. Cambridge, MA: Harvard University Press.

Ainsworth, M. (1973). The development of infant-mother attachment. In B. Caldwell & H. Ricciuti (Eds.), Review of child development research 3 (pp. 1-95). New York: Russell Sage Foundation.

Atkinson, M. (1992). Children's syntax: An introduction to principles and parameters theory. Oxford, UK: Blackwell.

Austin, J. (1962). How to do things with words. New York: Oxford University Press.

Bakhtin, M. (1981). The dialogic imagination: Four essays by M. M. Bakhtin. In M. Holquist (Ed.), trans. C. Emerson and M. Holquist. Austin, TX: University of Texas Press

Bakhtin, M. (1986). Speech genres and other late essays. In C. Emerson & M. Holquist (Eds.); trans. V. W. McGee. Austin, TX: University of Texas Press.

Bates, E., & MacWhinney, B. (1979). A functional approach to the acquisition of grammar. In E. Ochs & B. Schieffelin (Eds.), Developmental pragmatics (pp. 157-214). New York: Academic Press.

Baumeister, A. (1984). Some methodological and conceptual issues in the study of cognitive processes with retarded people. In P. Brooks, R. Sperber, & C. McCauley (Eds.), Learning and cognition in the mentally retarded (pp. 1-38). Hillsdale, NJ: Erlbaum.

Berk, L., & Winsler, B. (1995). Scaffolding children's learning: Vygotsky and early childhood education. NAEYC Research and Practice Series, 7. Washington, DC: National Association for the Education of Young Children.

160

Bever, T. (1992). The logical and extrinsic sources of modularity. In M. Gunner & M. Maratsos (Eds.), Modularity and constraints in language and cognition (pp. 179-212). Hillsdale, NJ: Erlbaum.

Bivens, J., & Berk, L. (1990). Longitudinal study of the development of elementary school children's private speech. Merrill-Palmer Quarterly, 36, 443-463.

Bivens, J. A., & Hagstrom, F. (1992). The representation of private speech in children's literature. In R. Diaz & L. Berk (Eds.) Private speech from social interaction to self-regulation (pp. 159-177). Hillsdale, NJ: Erlbaum.

Bloom, L. (1973). One word at a time. The Hague, Netherlands: Mouton.

Bloom, L., & Beckwith, R. (1988). Intentionality and language development. Unpublished manuscript, Columbia University Teachers College, New York.

Bloom, L., Beckwith, R., Capatides, J., & Hafitz, J. (1988). Expression through affect and words in the transition from infancy to language. In P. Baltes, D. Featherman, & R. Lerner (Eds.), Life-span development and behavior (Vol. 8, pp. 99-127). Hillsdale, NJ: Erlbaum.

Bloom, L., Hood, L., & Lightbown, P. (1974). Imitation in language development: If, when, and why. Cognitive Psychology, 6, 380-420.

Bloom, L., & Lahey, M. (1978). Language development and language disorders. New York: Wiley.

Bloom, L., Rispoli, M., Gartner, B., & Hafitz, J. (1989). Acquisition of complementation. Journal of Child Language, 16, 101-120.

Bodrova, E., & Leong, D. J. (1996). Tools of the mind. Columbus, OH: Merrill.

Boggiano, A., Shields, A., Barrett, M., Kellam, T., Thompson, E., Simons, J., & Katz, P. (1992). Helplessness deficits in students: The role of motivational orientation. Motivation and emotion, 16, 271-296.

Bohannon, J., & Bonvillian, J. (2001). Theoretical approaches to language acquisition. In J. Berko Gleason (Ed.), The development of language (5th ed., pp. 254-324). Boston: Allyn & Bacon.

Bowe, F. (Ed.)(1988). Toward equality: Education of the deaf. Commission on education of the deaf, Report to Congress and the President. Washington, DC: US Government Printing Office.

Bowlby, J. (1973). Attachment and loss. Vol. II: Separation. New York: Basic Books.

Boyer, E. (1988). Report card on school reform. New York: The Carnegie Foundation for the Advancement of Teaching.

Bronfenbrenner, U. (1974). Developmental research, public policy, and the ecology of childhood. Child Development, 45, 1-5.

Bronfenbrenner, U. (1979). The ecology of human development. Cambridge, MA: Harvard University Press.

Brown, R. (1956). Language and categories. In J. Bruner, J. Goodnow, & G. Austin (Eds.), A study of thinking (pp. 247-312). New York: Wiley.

Brown, R. (1973). A first language: The early stages. Cambridge, MA: Harvard University Press.

Brown, R. (1977). Introduction. In C. Snow & C. Ferguson (Eds.), Talking to children (pp. 1-27). New York: Cambridge University Press.

Brown, R. (1986). Social psychology (2nd ed.). New York: Free Press.

Brown, R., & Bellugi, U. (1963). Three processes in the child's acquisition of syntax. Harvard Educational Review, 34, 133-151.

Bruner, J. (1961). The act of discovery. Harvard Educational Review, 31, (1), 21-32.

Bruner, J. (1973). Beyond the information given. New York: Norton.

Bruner, J. (1975). The ontogenesis of speech acts. Journal of Child Language, 2, 1-19.

Bruner, J. (1978). Foreword. In A. Lock (Ed.), Action, gesture and symbol: The emergence of language, pp. vii-viii. New York: Academic Press.

Bruner, J. (1981). The social context of language acquisition. Language & Communication, 1, 155-178.

Bruner, J. (1986). Actual minds, possible worlds. Cambridge, MA: Harvard University Press.

Bruner, J. (1990). Acts of meaning. Cambridge, MA: Harvard University Press.

Caplow, J., & Kardash, C. (1995). Collaborative learning activies in graduate courses. Innovative Higher Education, 19, 207-221.

Cazden, C. (1965). Environmental assistance to the child acquisition of grammar. Unpublished doctoral dissertation. Harvard University.

Cazden, C. (1972). Child language and education. New York: Holt, Rinehart, & Winston.

Cazden C. (1988). Environmental assistance revisited: Variation and structural equivalence. In F. Kessel (Ed.), The development of language and language researchers (pp. 281-298). Hillsdale, NJ: Erlbaum.

Cazden, C. (1993). Vygotsky, Hymes, and Bakhtin: From word to utterance and voice. In E. Forman, N. Minick, & C. A. Stone (Eds.) Contexts for learning (pp. 197-212). Oxford, UK: Oxford University Press.

Center for Assessment and demographic studies (CADS). (1991). Stanford achievement test (8th ed.): Hearing-impaired norms. Gallaudet Research Institute, Gallaudet University.

Cheyne, J., & Tarulli, D. (1999). Dialogue, difference, and the "third voice" in the zone of proximal development. Theory and Psychology, 9, 5-28.

Chomsky, N. (1957). Syntactic structures. The Hague, Netherlands: Mouton.

Chomsky, N. (1959). Review of Skinner's Verbal Behavior. Language, 35, 26-58.

Chomsky, N. (1965). A transformational approach to syntax. In J. Fodor & J. Katz (Eds.), The structure of language (pp. 211-245). Englewood Cliffs, NJ: Prentice Hall.

Chomsky, N. (1968). Language and the mind. New York: Harcourt Brace Jovanovich.

Chomsky, N. (1982). Some concepts and consequences of the theory of government and binding. Cambridge, MA: MIT Press.

Clark, H., & Clark, E. (1977). Psychology and language. New York: Harcourt Brace Jovanovich.

Clarke-Stewart, K. (1973). Interactions between mothers and their young children: Characteristics and their consequences. Monographs: Society for Research in Child Development (No. 153).

Classroom Compass (1995). Constructing knowledge in the classroom. Classroom compass. 1, 3. <http://www.sedl.org/scimath/compass/v01n03/construct.html>.

Cloud, S. (1998). Multicultural language issues: A challenge for the future. American Speech-Language-Hearing Association Convention, San Antonio, TX.

Cloud, S., Buisson, J., & Hall, F. (2001). Multicultural language issues: Interacting effectively with individuals from Deaf Culture. American Speech-Language-Hearing Association Convention. New Orleans, LA.

Cloud, S., & Muma, J. (1999). Challenge for higher education: Teaching the cognitive social bases of language. Issues in Higher Education, 3, 3-5, 14-20.

Cole, L. (1989). E pluribus pluribus: Multicultural imperatives for the 1990s and beyond. Asha, 31, p. 67.

Conant, S. (1987). The relationship between age and MLU in young children: A second look at Klee and Fitzgerald's data. Journal of Child Language, 14, 169-173.

Condry, J. (1977). Enemies of exploration: Self-initiated versus other-initiated learning. Journal of personality and social psychology, 35, 459-477.

Costello, E. (2000). American sign language medical dictionary. New York: Random House.

Coulston, A. (1988). Hey listen! Deaf culture. Visual Communication Services, Inc.

Crain, W. (1992). Theories of development: Concepts and applications (3rd ed). Englewood Cliffs, NJ: Prentice Hall.

Cruickshank, W. (1972). Some issues facing the field of learning disabilities. Journal of Learning Disabilities, 5, 380-387.

Danner, F., & Lonky, E. (1981). A cognitive-developmental approach to the effects of rewards on intrinsic motivation. Child Development, 52, 1043-1052.

Davitz, J. (1966). The communication of emotional meaning. In A. Smith (Ed.), Communication and culture (pp. 467-480). New York: Holt, Rinehart, and Winston, Inc.

deCharms, R. (1972). Personal causation training in the schools. Journal of Applied Psychology, 2, 95-113.

De Tocqueville, A. (1840). Democracy in America. Cambridge, GA: Sever & Francis.

DeVries, R., Zan, B., Hildebrandt, C., Edmiaston, R., & Sales, C. (2002). Developing constructivist early childhood curriculum: Practical principles and activities. New York: Teachers College Press.

Dollard, N. (1996). Constructive classroom management. Focus on Exceptional Children, 29 (2), 1-12.

Donaldson, M. (1978). Children's minds. New York: Norton.

Dore, J. (1989). Monologue as reenvoicement of dialogue. In K. Nelson (Ed.), Narratives from the crib (pp. 231-260). Cambridge, MA: Harvard University Press.

Easterbrooks, S. (1999). Improving practices for students with hearing impairments. Exceptional Children, 65, 537-554.

Easterbrooks, S., & Baker, S. (2001). Language learning in children who are deaf and hard of hearing: Multiple pathways. Boston: Allyn & Bacon.

Ely, R. (1997). Language and literacy in the school years. In J. Berko Gleason (Ed.), The development of language, (pp. 398-439). Boston: Allyn & Bacon.

Fey, M. (1986). Language intervention with young children. San Diego, CA: College Hill Press.

Fodor, J. (1983). The modularity of the mind: An essay on faculty psychology. Cambridge, MA: MIT Press.

Forman, E., Minick, N., & Stone, C. (Eds.)(1993). Context for learning. Oxford, UK: Oxford University Press.

Furth, H. (1966). Thinking without language: Psychological implications of deafness. New York: Free Press.

Galin, J., & Latchaw, J. (Eds.). (1998). The dialogic classroom: Teachers integrating computer technology, pedagogy, and research. Urbana, IL: National Council of Teachers of English.

Gallagher, T. (1983). Pre-assessment: A procedure for accommodating language use variability. In T. Gallagher & C. Prutting (Eds.), Pragmatic assessment and intervention issues in language (pp. 1-28). San Diego: College-Hill Press.

Garmston, R., & Wellman, B. (1999). The adaptive school: A sourcebook for developing collaborative groups. Norwood, MA: Christopher-Gordon Publishers, Inc.

Garner, W. (1966). To perceive is to know. American Psychologist, 21, 11-19.

Geschwind, N. (1965a). Disconnexion syndromes in animals and man. Brain, 88, 237-294.

Geschwind, N. (1965b). Disconnexion syndromes in animals and man. Brain, 88, 585-644.

Glasser, W. (1990). The quality school: Managing students without coercion. New York: Harper Perennial.

Glasser, W. (1998). Quality school teacher. New York: Harper Perennial.

Gleitman, L. (1994). The structural sources of verb meanings. In P. Bloom (Ed.), Language acquisition: Some core readings (pp. 174-221). Cambridge, MA: MIT Press.

Gleitman, L., Gleitman, H., Landau, B., & Wanner, E. (1988). Where learning begins: Initial representations for language learning. In F. Newmeyer (Ed.), Linguistics: The Cambridge survey III: Language: Psychological and biological aspects (pp. 150-193). Cambridge, UK: Cambridge University Press.

Goldfield, B., & Snow, C. (2001). Individual differences: Implications for the study of language acquisition. In J. Berko Gleason (Ed.), The development of language (pp. 315-346). Boston: Allyn & Bacon.

Goldin-Meadow, S., & Mylander, C. (1984). Gestural communication in deaf children: The effects and noneffects of parental input on early language development. Monographs of the Society of Research in Child Development (Serial No. 207).

Goodlad, J. (1984). A place called school: Prospects for the future. New York: McGraw-Hill.

Goodman, K. (1986). What's whole in whole language? Portsmouth, NH: Heinemann.

Gould, J. (1996). A constructivist perspective on teaching and learning in the language arts. In C. Fosnot (Ed.), Constructivism: Theory, perspectives, and practice (pp. 92-102). New York: Teachers College Press.

Greenfield, P., & Smith, J. (1976). Communication and the beginnings of language. New York: Academic Press.

Grice, H. (1975). Logic and conversation. In P. Cole & J. Morgan (Eds.), Syntax and semantics: Vol. 3, Speech acts (pp. 41-58). New York: Seminar Press.

Grimshaw, J. (1981). Form, function, and the language acquisition device. In C. Baker & J. McCarthy (Eds.), The logical problem of language acquisition (pp. 183-210). Cambridge, MA: MIT Press.

Groht, M. (1958). Natural language for deaf children. Washington, DC: Alexander Graham Bell Association of the Deaf.

Grossman, H. (1995). Teaching in a diverse society. Boston, MA: Allyn & Bacon.

Guion, R. (1977). Content validity: Three years of talk—What's the action? Public Personnel Management, 6, 407-414.

Hagstrom, F. (2000). Mediated action analysis: A tool for planning zones of proximal development from standardized tests. Contemporary Issues in Communication Sciences and Disorders, 27 (2), 135-142.

Halliday, M. (1975). Learning how to mean. In E. Lenneberg & E. Lenneberg (Eds.), Foundations of language development: A multidisciplinary approach (pp. 239-266). New York: Academic Press.

Harris, Z. (1965). Co-occurrence and transformation in linguistic structure. In J. Fodor & J. Katz (Eds.), The structure of language (pp. 155-210). Englewood Cliffs, NJ: Prentice Hall.

Hart, T., & Risley, B. (1995). Meaningful differences in the everyday experience of young American children. Baltimore: Brooks.

Harvard School of Education (1971). Challenging the myths: The schools, the blacks, and the poor. Cambridge, MA: Harvard Educational Review.

Harvard School of Education (1973). The rights of children (Part 1). Cambridge, MA: Harvard Educational Review.

Harvard School of Education (1974). The rights of children (Part 2). Cambridge, MA: Harvard Educational Review.

Hicks, D. (Ed.). (1997). Discourse, learning, and schooling. Cambridge, UK: Cambridge University Press.

Higgins, P. (1980). Outsiders in a hearing world: A sociology of deafness. Beverly Hills, CA: Sage Publications.

Hobson, R. (2000). The grounding of symbols: A social-developmental account. In P. Mitchell & K. Riggs (Eds.), Children's reasoning and the mind (pp. 11-35). East Sussex, UK: Psychology Press Ltd, Publishers.

Hodson, (1986). Assessment of phonological processes—Revised. Danville, IL: Interstate Printers and Publishers.

Holquist, M. (2001). Personal communication.

Holt, J., Hotto, S., & Cole, K. (1994). Demographic aspects of hearing impairment: Questions and answers (3rd ed.). http://gri.gallaudet.edu/Demography/factsheet.html#Q1. Washington, DC: Center for Assessment and Demographic Studies, Gallaudet University.

Huang, R., Hopkins, J., & Nippold, M. (1998). Satisfaction with standardized language tests: A survey of speech language pathologists. Language, Speech, Hearing in Schools, 28, 12-23.

Hudson, J., & Fivush, R. (1990). Introduction: What young children remember and why. In R. Fivush & J. Hudson (Eds.), Knowing and remembering in young children (pp. 1-8). New York: Cambridge University Press.

Hunt, K. (1964). Grammatical structures written at three grade levels. National Council of Teachers of English (Research Report No. 1).

Hunt, R. (1994). Speech genres, writing genres, school genres, and computer genres. In A. Freedman & P. Medway (Eds.), Learning and the teaching genre (pp. 243-262). Portsmouth, NH: Boynton/Cook Publishers, Inc.

Ingram, D. (1989). First language acquisition: Method, description and explanation. New York: Cambridge University Press.

Johnson, R., Liddell, S., & Erting, C. (1989). Unlocking the curriculum: Principles for achieving access in deaf education. Gallaudet Research Institute Working Paper 89-3. Washington, DC: Gallaudet University.

Kagan, J. (1970). Determinants of attention in the infant. American Scientist, 56, 298-306.

Kagan, J., & Lewis, M. (1965). Studies of attention in the human infant. Merrill-Palmer Quarterly, 11, 95-127.

Kaplan, A. (1964). The conduct of inquiry: Methodology for behavioral science. San Francisco: Chandler.

Karmiloff-Smith, A. (1992). Beyond modularity. Cambridge, MA: MIT Press.

Kikas, E., & Hagstrom, F. (1993). Pensar con libertad de eleccion y en colaboracion: introduccion de la escritura en proceso en una escuela estonia. Communicacion, Lenguaje y Educacion, 19(20), 149-156.

Kirk, S., McCarthy, J., & Kirk, W. (1968). Illinois Test of Psycholinguistic Abilities (Rev. ed.). Urbana, IL: University of Illinois Press.

Kirsch, I., Jungeblut, A., Jenkins, L., & Kolstad, A. (1993). Adult literacy in America: A first look at the results of the National Adult Literacy Survey. Washington, DC: U.S. Department of Education.

Klee, T., & Fitzgerald, M. (1985). The relationship between grammatical development and mean length of utterance in morphemes. Journal of Child Language, 12, 251-269.

Kohn, A. (1993). Punished by rewards. Boston: Houghton Mifflin.

Kuczaj, S., & Barrett, M. (1986). The development of word meaning. New York: Springer-Verlag.

Lahey, M. (1988). Language disorders and language development. New York: Macmillan.

Lahey, M. (1994). Grammatical morpheme acquisition: Do norms exist? Journal of Speech and Hearing Research, 37, 1192-1194.

Lakoff, G. (1987). Women, fire, and dangerous things: What categories reveal about the mind. Chicago: University of Chicago Press.

Lane, H. (1989). When the mind hears: A history of the deaf. New York: Random House.

Lane, H. (1992). The mask of benevolence. New York: Alfred A. Knopf.

Lane, H., Hoffmeister, R., Behan, B. (1996). Journey into the deaf-world. San Diego, CA: Dawn Sign Press.

Langer, E. (1997). The power of mindful learning. New York: Addison-Wesley Publishing.

Lee L. (1974). Developmental sentence analysis. Evanston, IL: Northwestern University Press.

Lee, L., & Canter, S. (1971). Developmental sentence scoring: A clinical procedure for estimating syntactic development in children's spontaneous speech. Journal of Speech and Hearing Disorders, 36, 315-340.

Lepper, M., Greene, D., & Nisbett, R. (1973). Undermining children's intrinsic interest with extrinsic reward: A test of the "overjustification" hypothesis. Journal of Personality and Social Psychology, 28, 129-137.

Leonard, L. (1987). Is specific language impairment a useful construct? In S. Rosenberg (Ed.), Advances in applied psycholinguistics. I. Disorders of first language development (pp. 1-39). New York: Cambridge University Press.

Leonard, L. (1989). Language learnability and specific language impairment in children. Applied Psycholinguistics, 10, 179-202.

Lieberman, L. (2001). The death of special education: Having the right to fail in regular education is no entitlement. Education Week, January 17.

Lightfoot, D. (1989). The child's trigger experience: Degree-0 learnability. Behavioral and Brain Sciences, 12, 321-375.

Lock, A. (1978)(Ed.), Action, gesture and symbol. New York: Academic Press.

Loritz, D. (1999). How the brain evolved language. New York: Oxford University Press.

Lotmann, Y. M. (1988). Text within a text. Soviet Psychology, 26(3), 32-51.

Lust, B. (1986a). Studies in the acquisition of anaphora (Vol. 1). Boston: Reidel.

Lust, B. (1986b). Studies in the acquisition of anaphora (Vol. 2). Boston: Reidel.

MacIver, D.J., & Epstein, J.L. (1994). Impact of algebra-focused course content and active learning/teaching for understanding instructional approaches on eighth-graders' achievement. Baltimore, MD: Johns Hopkins University Center for Social Organization of Schools.

Macken, M. (1987). Representation, rules, and overgeneralization in phonology. In B. MacWhinney (Ed.), Mechanisms of language acquisition (pp. 367-397). Hillsdale, NJ: Erlbaum.

Mandler, J. (1978). A code in the node: The use of a story schema in retrieval. Discourse Processes, 1, 14-35.

Mandler, J. (1979). Commentary: A trilogue on dialogue. In M. Bornstein & W. Kessen (Eds.), Psychological development from infancy (pp. 373-382). Hillsdale, NJ: Erlbaum.

Mandler, J. (1983). Representation. In P. Mussen (Series Ed.), & J. Flavell & E. Markman (Vol. Eds.), Handbook of child psychology: Vol. 3. Cognitive development, 4th ed. (pp. 420-494). New York: Wiley.

Marlowe, B., & Page, M. (1998). Creating and sustaining the constructivist classroom. Thousand Oaks, CA: Corwin Press, Inc.

Martin, E. (1980). [Correspondence to ASHA (Stan Dublinski) regarding the official interpretation of P.L. 94-142]. Washington, DC: U.S. Department of Health, Education, and Welfare.

Martin, L., Nelson, K., & Tobach, E. (Eds.) (1995). Sociocultural psychology. Cambridge, UK: Cambridge University Press.

Mayer, C., & Wells, G. (1996). Can the linguistic interdependence theory support a bilingual-bicultural model of literacy education for deaf students? Journal of Deaf Studies and Deaf Education, 1(2), 93-107.

McAnally, P., Rose, S., Quigley, S. (1994). Language learning practices with deaf children (2nd ed.). Austin, TX: PRO-ED.

McClelland, J., & Rumelhart, D. (Eds.). (1986). Parallel distributed processing: Explorations in the microstructure of cognition. Cambridge, MA: MIT Press.

McNeill, D. (1966). Developmental psycholinguistics. In F. Smith & G. Miller (Eds.), The genesis of language (pp. 15-84). Cambridge, MA: MIT Press.

Medlin, D., & Ross, B. (1992). Cognitive Psychology. New York: Harcourt Brace Jovanovich.

Meier, R. (1991, January & February). Language acquisition by deaf children. American Scientist, 60-70.

Mercer, J. (1972). The lethal label. Psychology Today, 6, 44-47, 95-97.

Mercer, J. (1974). A policy statement on assessment procedures and the rights of children. Harvard Educational Review, 44, 125-142.

Merriam-Webster (1974). Webster's New Collegiate Dictionary (p. 708). Springfield, MA: G. & C. Merriam Company.

Messick, S. (1975). The standard problem: Meaning and values in measurement and evaluation. American Psychologist, 30, 955-966.

Messick, S. (1980). Test validity and the ethics of assessment. American Psychologist, 35, 1012-1027.

Messick, S. (1989). Validity. In R. Linn (Ed.), Educational measurement (pp. 13-103). New York: Macmillan.

Messick, S. (1995). Validity of psychological assessment. American Psychologist, 50, 741-749.

Miller, J. (2001). Why aren't you using language sample analysis? Even when you know you should... ASHA Leader.

Miller, J., & Chapman, R. (1981). The relationship between age and mean length of utterance in morphemes. Journal of Speech and Hearing Research, 24, 154-161.

Moll, L. (Ed.) (1990). Vygotsky and education. Cambridge, UK: Cambridge University Press.

Mueller, A., & Fleming, T. (2001). Cooperative learning: Listening to how children work at school. Journal of Educational Research, 94, 259-265.

Muma, J. (1971). Language intervention: Ten techniques. Language, Speech, and Hearing Services in Schools, 5, 7-17.

Muma, J. (1978). Language handbook. Englewood Cliffs, NJ: Prentice Hall.

Muma, J. (1981). Language primer. Lubbock, TX: Natural Child.

Muma, J. (1983). Speech-language pathology: Emerging clinical expertise in language. In T. Gallagher & C. Prutting (Eds.), Pragmatic assessment and intervention issues in language (pp. 195-214). San Diego, CA: College-Hill.

Muma, J. (1986). Language acquisition: A functionalistic perspective. Austin, TX: PRO-ED.

Muma, J. (1991). Experiential cognition: Clinical implications. In T. Gallagher (Ed.), Pragmatics of language (pp. 229-247). San Diego, CA: Singular.

Muma, J. (1998). Effective speech-language pathology: A cognitive socialization approach. Mahwah, NJ: Erlbaum.

Muma, J. (2000). Toward a viable definition of specific language impairment (unpublished).

Muma, J. (forthcoming). Construct validity: The essence of language assessment.

Muma, J., & Brannon, C. (1986). Language sampling. Miniseminar, American Speech-Language-Hearing Association Convention (miniseminar).

Muma, J., Morales, A., Day, K., Tackett, A., Smith, S., Daniel, B., Logue, B., & Morriss, D. (1998). Language sampling: Grammatical assessment. In Muma, J., Effective speech-language pathology: A cognitive socialization approach (pp. 310-345). Mahwah, NJ: Erlbaum.

Muma, J., & Teller, H. (2000). Intent: The centrality of language. 26th Annual Conference of Association of Educators: Deaf/Hard of Hearing. New Orleans.

Muma, J., & Teller, H. (2001). Developments in cognitive socialization: Implications for deaf education. American Annals of the Deaf, 146, 31-38.

Nash, J. (2000). Shifting stigma from body to self: Paradoxical consequences of mainstreaming. In P. Spencer, C. Erting, & M. Marsscharh (Eds.), The deaf child in the family and at school (pp. 211-227). Mahwah, NJ: Erlbaum.

Nelson, K. (1985). Making sense. The acquisition of shared meaning. New York: Academic Press.

Nelson, K. (1986). Event knowledge: Structure and function in development. Hillsdale, NJ: Erlbaum.

Nelson, K. (1990). Event knowledge and the development of language functions. In J. Miller (Ed.), Research on child language disorders. New York: Little, Brown.

Nelson, K. (1996). Language in cognitive development. New York: Cambridge University Press.

Ninio, A., Snow, C., Pan, B., & Rollins, P. (1994). Classifying communicative acts in children's interactions. Journal of Communication Disorders, 27, 157-187.

Nuru-Holm, N., & Battle, D. E. (1998). Multicultural aspects of Deafness. In D. E. Battle (Ed.), Communication disorders in multicultural populations (2nd ed.) (pp. 355-377). Newton, MA: Butterworth-Heinemann.

Olson, D., & Bruner, J. (1996). Folk psychology and folk pedagogy. In D. Olson & N. Torrance (Eds.), The handbook of education and human development: New models of learning, teaching and schooling. Cambridge, MA: Blackwell.

Osgood, C. (1957). Motivational dynamics of language behavior. Nebraska Symposium on Motivation. Lincoln, NE: University of Nebraska Press.

Palincsar, A., & Brown, A. (1984). Reciprocal teaching of comprehension fostering and comprehension monitoring. Cognition and Instruction, 1 (2), 117-75.

Paul, P., & Quigley, S. (1990). Education and deafness. White Plains, NY: Longman.

Paul, P., & Jackson, D. (1993). Toward a psychology of deafness. Boston: Allyn and Bacon.

Paul, P. (2001). Language and deafness (3rd ed.). San Diego, CA: Singular.

Paul, R. (1995). Language disorders from infancy through adolescence. St. Louis, MO: Mosby Yearbook.

Pelley, S. (April, 2000). Birth of a language: Children without language so they invent one of their own. 60 Minutes II. CBS Worldwide, Inc. Retrieved from the World Wide Web: http://www.cbsnews.cbs.com.

Perera, K. (1994). Editorial: Child language research: Building on the past, looking to the future. Journal of Child Language, 21, 1-7.

Piaget, J. (1926). The language and thought of the child. New York: Harcourt, Brace.

Piaget, J. (1955). Language and thought of a child. New York: World Publishing.

Piaget, J. (1973). Child and reality. New York: Grossman.

Pinker, S. (1984). Language learnability and language development. Cambridge, MA: Harvard University Press.

Pinker, S. (1987). The bootstrapping problem in language acquisition. In B. MacWhinney (Ed.), Mechanisms of language acquisition (pp. 399-442). Hillsdale, NJ: Erlbaum.

Pinker, S. (1988). Learnability theory and the acquisition of a first language. In F. Kessel (Ed.), The development of language and language researchers (pp. 97-120). Hillsdale, NJ: Erlbaum.

Plante, E. (1998). Criteria for SLI: The Stark and Tallal legacy and beyond. Journal of Speech, Language, and Hearing Research, 41, 951-957.

Priestley, T. (1980). Homonymy in child phonology. Journal of Child Psychology, 7, 413–427.

Prutting, C., Epstein, L., Beckman, S., Dias, I., & Gao, X. (1989). Inquiry into and tampering with nature: A clinical perspective. Unpublished manuscript. University of California—Santa Barbara.

Ratner, N. (2001). Atypical language development. In J. Gleason (Ed.), The development of language (pp. 347-408). Boston: Allyn & Bacon.

Renfrew, C. (1966). Persistence of the open syllable in defective articulation. Journal of Speech and Hearing Disorders, 31, 370-373.

Rees, N., & Snope, J. (1983). National conference on undergraduate, graduate, and continuing education. Asha, 25, 49-59.

Rice, M., Buhr, J., & Nemeth, M. (1990). Fast mapping word-learning abilities of language-delayed preschoolers. Journal of Speech and Hearing Disorders, 55, 33-42.

Rice, M., Haney, K., & Wexler, K. (1989). Family histories of children with SLI who show extended optional infinitives. Journal of Speech, Language, and Hearing Research, 41, 419-432.

Rice, M., Wexler, K., & Hershberger, S. (1998). Tense over time: The longitudinal course of tense acquisition in children with specific language impairment. Journal of Speech, Language, and Hearing Research, 41, 1412-1431.

Rogoff, B. (1990). Apprenticeship in thinking: Cognitive development in social context. New York: Oxford University Press.

Rommetveit, R. (1992). Outlines of a dialogically based social-cognitive approach to human cognition and communication. In A. Wold (Ed.), The dialogical alternative (pp. 19-44). Oslo, Norway: Scandinavian University Press.

Rosch, E. (1973). Natural categories. Cognitive Psychology, 4, 328-350.

Rosner, J. (2001). Parent and teacher guide for children who fail school. Houston, TX: University of Houston Eye Institute.

Rutter, M. (1979). Maternal deprivation, 1972–1978: New findings, new concepts, new approaches. Child Development, 50, 283–305.

Schiavetti, N., & Metz, D. (1997). Evaluating research in communicative disorders (3rd ed.). Boston, MA: Allyn & Bacon.

Schildroth, A., & Hotto, S. (1993). Annual survey of hearing impaired children and youth: 1989-90 school year. American Annals of the Deaf, 136, 155-163.

Schirmer, B. (2000). Language and literacy development in children who are deaf (2nd ed.). Boston: Allyn & Bacon.

Schleper, D. (1995). Reading to deaf children: Learning from deaf adults. Washington, DC: Gallaudet University Laurent Clerc Center.

Schwartz, B. (1982). Reinforcement-induced behavioral stereotyping: How not to teach people to discover rules. Journal of Experimental Psychology, 111, 23-59.

Schwartz, R., & Leonard, L. (1982). Do children pick and choose? An examination of phonological selection and avoidance in early lexical acquisition. Journal of Child Language, 9, 319-336.

Searle, J. (1969). Speech acts: An essay in the philosophy of language. Cambridge, UK: Cambridge University Press.

Searle, J. (1983). Intentionality: An essay in the philosophy of the mind. Cambridge, UK: Cambridge University Press.

Searle, J. (1992). The rediscovery of the mind. Cambridge, MA: MIT Press.

Sidorkin, A. (1999). Beyond discourse. Albany, NY: State University of New York Press.

Sperber, D., & Wilson, D. (1986). Relevance: Communication and cognition. Cambridge, MA: Harvard University Press.

Stark, R., & Tallal, P. (1981). Selection of children with specific language deficits. Journal of Speech and Heaing Disorders, 46, 114-122.

Stewart, D., & Kluwin, T. (2001). Teaching deaf and hard of hearing students. Boston: Allyn & Bacon.

Tager-Flusberg, H., & Cooper, J. (1999). Present and future possibilities for defining a phenotype for specific language impairment. Journal of Speech, Language, and Hearing Research, 42, 1275-1278.

Tallal, P. (1990). Fine-grained discrimination deficits in language-learning impaired children are specific neither to the auditory modality nor to speech perception. Journal of Speech and Hearing Research, 33, 616-617.

Teller, H., & Harriss, C. (1991). Getting to know you (and teach you to write) through the dialogue journal. Association Magazine of the British Association of Teachers of the Deaf.

Tucker, B. (1999). Cochlear implants. Jefferson, NC: McFarland 7 Company, Inc., Publishers.

Tunkis, G. (1963). Linguistic theory in the transformational approach. Lingua, 16, 364-376.

Tyack, D., & Gottsleben, R. (1977). Language sampling, analysis and training. (Rev. ed.). Palo Alto, CA: Consulting Psychologists Press.

U.S. Census Bureau (March 12, 2001). http://www.census.gov/ population/cen2000/phc-t1/tab01.txt.

Uzgiris, I., & Hunt, J. (1975). Assessment in infancy. Chicago: University of Illinois Press.

Vacca, R., & Raisinski, T. (1992). Case studies in Whole Language. Orlando, FL: Harcourt Brace Jovanovich.

Vander Woude, K. W. (1970). Problem solving and language. Archives of General Psychiatry, 23, 337-342.

Ventry, I., & Schiavetti, N. (1986). Evaluating research in speech pathology and audiology (2nd ed.). New York: Macmillan.

Vernon, M., & Andrews, J. (1990). The psychology of deafness: Understanding deaf and hard-of-hearing people. White Plains, NY: Longman.

Vihman, M., & Greenlee, M. (1987). Individual differences in phonological development: Ages one and three years. Journal of Speech and Hearing Research, 30, 503-521.

Vygotsky, L. (1962). Thought and language. Cambridge, MA: MIT Press.

Vygotsky, L. (1978). Mind in society: the development of higher psychological processes. In M. Cole, V. John-Steiner, S. Scribner, & E. Souberman (Eds.). Cambridge, MA: Harvard University Press.

Vygotsky, L. (1934/1987). Thinking and speech (trans. N. Minick). In R. Rieber & A. Carton (Eds.). The collected works of L. S. Vygotsky, Volume 1. New York: Plenum Press.

Vygotsky, L. (1983/1993). The fundamentals of defectology (trans. J. Knox & C. Stevens). In R. Rieber & A. Carton (Eds.) The collected works of L. S. Vygotsky, Volume 2. New York: Plenum Press.

Wanner, E. (1988). The parser's architecture. In F. Kessel (Ed.), The development of language and language researchers (pp. 79-96). Hillsdale, NJ: Erlbaum.

Watkins, R., & Rice, M. (1991). Verb particle and preposition acquisition in language impaired preschoolers. Journal of Speech and Hearing Research, 34, 1130-1141.

Watson, J. (1919). Psychology from the standpoint of a behaviorist (1st ed.). Philadelphia, PA: Lippencott.

Webster's New World Dictionary, College Edition (1968). New York: The World Publishing Co.

Weir, R. (1962). Language in the crib. The Hague, Netherlands: Mouton.

Welman, S., & Gelman, S. (1992). Cognitive development: Foundational theories of core domains. Annual Review of Psychology, 43, 337-375.

Wertsch, J. (1985). Vygotsky and the social formation of mind. Cambridge, MA: Harvard University Press.

Wertsch, J. (1991). Voices of the mind. Cambridge, MA: Harvard University Press.

Wertsch, J. (1998). Mind in action. Oxford, UK: Oxford University Press.

Wertsch, J., & Rupert, L. (1993). The authority of cultural tools in a sociocultural approach to mediated agency. Cognition and Instruction, 11, 3-4, 227-239.

Wertsch, J., Tulviste, P., & Hagstrom, F. (1993). A sociocultural approach to agency. In E. Forman, N. Minick, & A. Stone (Eds.), Context for learning. Oxford, UK: Oxford University Press.

Wexler, K. (1994). Optional infinatives, head movement and the economy of derivations. In N. Hornstein & D. Lightfoot (Eds.), Verb movement. Cambridge, UK: Cambridge University Press.

White, A., Scott, P., & Grant, D. (2002). Structural analysis of basal readers using words per T-unit and morphemes per T-unit as the primary units of analysis. Volta Review, 102, 87-98.

Wong, H., & Wong, C. (1998). How to become an effective teacher: The first days of school. Thousand Oaks, CA: Harry K. Wong Publishing Co.

Yates, J.R. (1988). Demography as it affects special education. In A. Ortiz, & B. Ramirez (Eds.), Schools and the culturally diverse exceptional student: Promising practices and future directions (pp. 1-4). Reston, VA: The Council for Exceptional Children.

Zak, O. (1995). Strategies for communication between the hearing and the hearing-impaired. http://www.zak.com/deaf-info/old/comm_strategies.html